THE LORD'S PRAYER

By:

HENRY J. VAN DYKE
PASTOR OF THE FIRST PRESBYTERIAN CHURCH, BROOKLYN, N.Y.

WIPF & STOCK · Eugene, Oregon

Wipf and Stock Publishers
199 W 8th Ave, Suite 3
Eugene, OR 97401

The Lord's Prayer
By Van Dyke, Henry J.
Softcover ISBN-13: 978-1-7252-9139-3
Hardcover ISBN-13: 978-1-7252-9138-6
eBook ISBN-13: 978-1-7252-9140-9
Publication date 5/1/2021
Previously published by Robert Carter and Brothers, 1871

This edition is a scanned facsimile of
the original edition published in 1871.

THE LORD'S PRAYER.

MATT. vi. 7-13.

BUT when ye pray, use not vain repetitions, as the heathen *do:* for they think that they shall be heard for their much speaking.

8. Be not ye therefore like unto them: for your Father knoweth what things ye have need of before ye ask him.

9. After this manner therefore pray ye: Our Father which art in heaven, Hallowed be thy name.

10. Thy kingdom come. Thy will be done in earth, as *it is* in heaven.

11. Give us this day our daily bread.

12. And forgive us our debts, as we forgive our debtors.

13. And lead us not into temptation, but deliver us from evil. For thine is the kingdom, and the power, and the glory, for ever. Amen.

LUKE xi. 1-4.

AND it came to pass, that, as he was praying in a certain place, when he ceased, one of his disciples said unto him, Lord, teach us to pray, as John also taught his disciples.

2. And he said unto them, When ye pray, say, Our Father which art in heaven, Hallowed be thy name. Thy kingdom come. Thy will be done, as in heaven, so in earth.

3. Give us day by day our daily bread.

4. And forgive us our sins; for we also forgive every one that is indebted to us. And lead us not into temptation; but deliver us from evil.

"AND when ye pray, be not garrulous like the heathen; for they expect to be heard for their abundance of words. Therefore be not like them, for your Father knoweth what is needful for you before ye ask him. In this manner therefore pray ye: Our father which art in heaven, hallowed be thy name: thy kingdom come: thy will be done, as in heaven, so in earth. Give us our needful bread this day; and forgive us our debts as we forgive our debtors; and bring us not into temptation, but deliver us from evil; for thine is the kingdom, and the power, and the glory, for ever and ever. Amen."

Murdock's Translation of the Syriac Testament.

INTRODUCTION.

THE Lord's prayer is both a form and a model. As a form it is equally adapted to private and to public worship. It ought to be taught to little children among the first lessons of devotion. But it should not be put aside with childish things. No degree of intelligence or fervor can render it unsuitable. It ought to be repeated at the family altar and in the public assemblies of the church. To a mind unprejudiced by the abuses of superstition and formalism such frequent use of it would naturally be suggested by reverence for the wisdom and authority of its divine Author; even though the precept "*when ye pray say,*" prefixed to its second delivery (see Luke xi. 1), is not to be accepted in its most literal sense. The voluntary use of the Lord's prayer on all suitable occasions does no violence to the injunction with which it stands connected in the

Sermon on the Mount: " When ye pray use not vain repetitions as the heathen do: for they think they shall be heard for their much speaking." It has been well observed by one of the most eminent commentators of the Church of England that " what is forbidden in this precept is not *much praying*, for our Lord himself passed whole nights in prayer; nor praying *in the same words*, for this he did in the very intensity of his agony in Gethsemane; but making number and length *a point of observance*, and imagining that prayer will be heard, not because it is the genuine expression of the desire of faith, but because it is of such length and has been such a number of times repeated. The repetitions of Paternosters in the Romish Church are in direct violation of this precept; the *number* of repetitions being *prescribed*, and the *efficacy of the performance made to depend on it.* But the repetitions of the Lord's prayer in the Liturgy of the Church of England is not a violation of it, because it is not the number of these which is the object, but each has its appropriate place and season in what is pre-eminently a reasonable service."*
We have no disposition to controvert what is

* Alford.

here said about the service of the Church of England. But, for the sake of those who prefer the more free and pliable forms of worship adopted by non-Episcopal churches, we insist that the frequent voluntary use of the Lord's prayer gives no sanction to the claims of an enforced Liturgy. It is admitted on all sides that there is no evidence in Scripture or elsewhere that any Liturgy, with or without this prayer, was ever used by Christ or his apostles, or by their immediate successors. The gospel history records many prayers, all of which were occasional and extemporaneous; but there is no trace of a repetition of the form the Saviour twice gave to his disciples. The writer before quoted, though a devoted advocate of liturgical forms, frankly admits that the variations in the second delivery of the Lord's prayer, however unimportant in themselves, are fatal to the supposition of its being used liturgically at the time when these Gospels were written. And he adds, with the same creditable candor, that there is no trace of such liturgical use in any writer before the third century. Justin Martyr in his apology for Christianity, written at the close of the second century, says : " Every pastor offers up prayers and thanksgiving *to the best of his ability.*" The obvious meaning of which is, that every pastor prayed *extemporaneously;* not indeed without premeditation and that preparation of the heart and answer of the tongue which are from God, but without any fixed form, prepared beforehand, and to be used on all occasions. But, in perfect consistency with the habit of praying according to the best ability of him who led the worship, we know, from historic testimony equally conclusive, that it was customary in the earliest ages of the church to repeat the Lord's prayer at the beginning or at the conclusion of their own extemporaneous utterances. And this is the voluntary use of this divinely inspired form for which we now contend, as consistent alike with the freedom of the gospel and a due reverence for the wisdom and authority of our Great Teacher.

But the formal use of the Lord's prayer, in the repetition of the same words, does not fulfil the highest end for which it was given. It is the prayer of prayers, not because of any divine virtue residing in the words, or any exclusive power to prevail with God connected with the repetition of them. Neither does its value depend only upon its inspired adaptation to the desires of a devout and believing heart. It has a still higher use. Its worth is eminently due to its design and fitness as a MODEL PRAYER. When it first fell from the lips of the incarnate Word, and was set up by him in sublime contrast with the vain repetitions of the heathen, it was recommended by the precept, " After this manner therefore pray ye." And we think the ambiguous phrase *after this manner*, or, as it might be more briefly translated, *thus pray ye*, was purposely chosen, so as to include both the repetition of the same words, and the utterance of similar petitions modelled upon and inspired by them. It is not only to be repeated, but imitated. It is both a specimen to be used, and a pattern to be copied, according to the discretion and ability of every worshipper. It is a divine mould in which the substance of all Scripture doctrine and promises may be fashioned into multiform prayers. It is a sacred cartoon drawn by the hand of the divine Master, which every disciple may transfer to his own heart and fill up out of his own knowledge and experience. It is a fountain of light and love from which every worshipper may imbibe the spirit of grace and supplications. When we are conscious of our inability to lead the devotions of the sanctuary or the social circle, or even to pray for ourselves to our Father which seeth in secret, — and who does not feel that " we know not what we should pray for as we ought?" — let us sit down here at the feet of Christ; and he, by his word and spirit, will help our infirmities, and teach us how to pray. Interpreting this pattern in the light of all the Scriptures, and under the promptings of our own gracious experience, we may make our own hearts a living liturgy. Every word of this prayer is a lump of virgin gold. Every sentiment is a rich distilled perfume from the heart of the great Intercessor. Let us appropriate and coin these apples of gold and lay them up among our treasures in heaven. Let us imbue our whole nature with the savor of these good ointments, so that the desires of our heart, and the corresponding words of our mouth before God, may be put into the "golden vials full of odors which are the prayers of saints." (Rev. i. 8.) Let the sublime doctrines embodied in this prayer, the sweet but lofty devotion which pervades it, and the brief but comprehensive simplicity of its language, be our encouragement, our model, and our inspiration, in every approach to the throne of grace. So shall we realize and justify Tertullian's apology, written in the second century: "Christians pray with outspread, because clean hands; with uncovered head, because they are not ashamed; and without the aid of a prompter, because we pray from the heart."

THE MODEL PRAYER.

CHAPTER I.

"*Our Father which art in Heaven.*"

"THE Lord's prayer," says Matthew Henry, "as indeed every prayer, is a letter sent from earth to heaven. Here is the name of the person to whom it is sent, *our Father;* the place where, *in heaven;* the contents of it, in several errands of request; the close, *for thine is the kingdom;* the seal, *Amen;* and, if you will, the date too, *this day.*"

The theme of our present meditation is the inscription of the letter, in which three things claim our notice: the title given to God, *Father;* the appropriation of God as *our* father; and the place assigned to him, *in heaven.*

I. The idea that God is the father of his intelligent creatures is not peculiar to the

Scriptures. The desire to stand in a filial relation to the Supreme Being is among the deepest yearnings of the human heart. Even the heathen have claimed a divine original. "Certain also of their own poets have said, 'For we are also his offspring.'" And yet what heathen poets said was more a poetic fancy than a well-grounded assurance of the truth. It was sustained, not by an elevation of the creature to a conscious relationship to the Creator, but by changing the glory of the incorruptible God into an image made like to corruptible man. The father of gods and of men, as described in the Greek and Roman Mythology, was a being of like passions with his worshippers, and differed but little in character and authority from an earthly king. And he was but one of ten thousand deities by whose conflicting authority and caprices human destiny was supposed to be controlled. It was easy to claim kindred with such gods; but the claim could bring neither strength nor comfort to the soul. The incarnate Word of God, who came forth from the bosom of the Father to declare him, realizes to us that which uninspired reason has cherished as a poetic fancy; and, while he vindicates the glory of the Incorruptible and Eternal One from all the aspersions of the heathen, elevates men into a consciousness of a filial relationship to their Maker. The opening words of our Lord's prayer, embracing in the fulness of its meaning whatever the Bible teaches concerning the divine character, rises above all the conceptions of heathen poets concerning the origin and destiny of men as the children of the Highest. It is no less exalted above the modern pantheistic errors which effectively deny the existence of the Eternal One by identifying him with the human soul or with the works of his own hands. It is to no vague generalization of abstract qualities or forces, to no mere embodiment of the better qualities of our own nature, to no mere creature of human imagination, but to a living, personal, and true God, we are taught to apply the endearing appellation of Father. And the use of this title in prayer is not only founded on divine revelation, but it indicates an advanced stage in the application of revealed truth to human experience. In the Old Testament God is nowhere addressed as our Father; except in the single passage where the evangelical prophet, in anticipation of the coming Messiah, breaks forth in the exclamation: "Doubtless thou art our Father, though Abraham be ignorant of us and Israel acknowledge us not; thou O Lord art our Father, our Redeemer." The initial word of this prayer marks it, therefore, as belonging to the new rather than to the old economy. It presupposes the consciousness of an adoption, which gives to those of whom Abraham is ignorant a right to call God their Father, because he is their Redeemer. It is part of the grace and truth which came by Jesus Christ, and not of the law which was given by Moses. The great Prophet of the New Testament taught it to his own disciples. And he put this claim to a filial relationship with God into their heart and lips, not merely because they were dependent creatures, nor because they were children of Abraham, — all of which they might be and still come under the terrible censure, "Ye are of your father the devil," since "without faith the devil can show as good a coat of arms as we;" but because he had already endued them with the spirit of adoption and "given them power to become the sons of God." And this is the high privilege of all who receive and rest upon Christ for salvation. We stand before God, not upon the same footing with Adam, when amid the yet untainted bloom of Paradise he poured out his heart's gratitude to the bountiful Creator; nor on the same footing with angels who have kept their first estate; but, as fallen and redeemed sinners, we are "the children of God by faith in Christ Jesus." He through whom we have received the adoption of sons bids us claim kindred with God. How profound is the meaning of the simple words he gives us, to introduce our petitions! They reach down to the depths of our conscious wants, and up to the height of our divinest aspirations, and embrace every argument by which nature or revelation encourages our faith and gives us power to prevail with God. Whatever illustrations of the Creator's goodness may be found in the works of his hand, and whatever demonstrations of his grace are set forth in the greater work of redemption, are concentrated and brought vividly to mind whenever a Christian believingly says *our Father*. God has many sublime and expressive titles. His name proclaimed from the cleft of the rock, when Moses said, " I beseech thee shew me thy glory," was full of incomprehensible majesty and grace. The door-posts of the temple might well be moved when in the sublime vision of Isaiah the seraphim veiled their faces with their wings, and cried, " Holy, holy is the Lord of hosts." Angels, excelling in strength and conscious of perfect purity, delight in these lofty ascriptions. We, too, would exalt the Lord our God; ascribing to him every title of honor and glory the heart can conceive, or the tongue declare. And yet, amid this array of glowing names, the one Christ has taught us lingers upon our hearts and lips with a fond familiarity peculiar to itself. To us, in our frailty and sin, it is the most precious of all the divine titles. Amid the mingled joy and sorrow of our human relationships our own hearts interpret its meaning. When our children come to us with the name of father on their tongue, and the sweet confidence of childhood in their heart and face, we feel that we can withhold no good thing from them. When they are sick, we would give our own life to redeem them from the grave. When, through weakness or inexperience, they fall into danger, our heart melts with inexpressible pity. When they are wayward and disobedient, the rod which corrects them for their good falls more heavily upon ourselves. And can we not learn, from all this paternal experience, what Christ means when he teaches us to address God by the endearing name of Father? Surely he means us to believe that the Holy and Just One has turned away his anger from us; that the Almighty and Omniscient One will supply all our wants; that he pities our infirmities; that he will instruct and guide us in the way we should go; that he will have mercy on our unrighteousness, and even when he visits our iniquities with stripes will still embrace us in his everlasting love. Well may we exclaim with Chrysostom: "How wonderful is God's philanthropy! that one who is earthly is commanded to claim a heavenly, a mortal to claim an immortal, a corruptible to claim an incorruptible, a child of time to claim an eternal Father; that you, who but two or three days ago were nothing more than clay, are commanded to claim as father Him who is, from everlasting to everlasting, God!"

II. It is a simple but profound observation that the possessive pronouns, though among the smallest, are the most expressive words in the Bible. They bring the things which are unseen and eternal home to us. Every child knows the difference between *a* father and his own father. He goes to his own with a freedom and confidence no other one can inspire. Every Christian knows the immeasurable difference between the vague sentiment which regards God as in some sense the Father of the Universe, and that spirit of adoption by which we approach him in the assurance that he is *our* Father. Faith is genuine and precious only so far as it is appropriating. We are to receive Christ as our personal Teacher and Saviour. In the exercise of this personal trust we must come to God and appropriate him as our Father, and feel that we have an individual interest in him, and that —

> " We are as much his care as if, beside,
> No man or angel lived in earth or heaven."

But this individuality must be neither selfish nor exclusive. In the Lord's prayer the possessive pronoun is in the plural number. Not *my*, but *our* Father. And this indicates that our interest in God is shared by others with whom we are associated. It is not shared in the sense that it is divided. The sun is a whole sun to each one of the millions who behold its glory and rejoice in its light. So

God our Father bestows himself in his fulness upon each and all of his children. The Lord's prayer teaches us to remember that there are other children besides ourselves, and especially to recognize and feel this in the sacred moments when we draw near to God. "If faith utters the word Father, *love*, without which faith cannot be, immediately associates it with *our* Father, that all its prayer may go into the great fellowship of supplication and all its petitioning be intercession also."* Prayer indeed has a peculiar sweetness, and may plead the promise of a special blessing, when it is a social exercise. How precious at the family altar is the name of our heavenly Father! It puts the whole household, even the infant of days, under the shadow of the Almighty, and links all together in the circle of his gracious covenant. How good and pleasant a thing it is, when two or three assemble and agree in Christ's name as touching any thing they shall ask, or when a whole congregation are together with one accord in one place, for one to stand up before God, as the representative of all, and present their common supplications to "our Father." Nor is this recognition of others appropriate

* Steir.

only to the occasions when they are present with us before God. When we enter into our closet, and shut the door, we are to say "*our* Father." In our most solitary and secret addresses to him, we are but one of a great praying brotherhood, scattered through all time and over all the earth: we are kin to all who have ever prayed in the exercise of like precious faith. Paul and Silas in the midnight dungeon, Elias on the summit of Carmel, Moses on the Mount of Communion, Jacob wrestling and prevailing with the angel of the covenant, are all our relatives; and at the mercy-seat we claim the honor and the benefit of the connection. Especially when we pray to God as our Father, we remind him and ourselves of all those praying ones in whose affections we have had a peculiar interest; we take again the prayers in our behalf which once fell often and fervently from lips we loved, — now, alas! sealed and cold to us, — and we rehearse them before our fathers' God, and put them once more into the golden censer. Isaac prayed to the God of Abraham; thus claiming an interest in his father's covenant, and a blessing from his father's prayers. Jacob called upon the God of Abraham and of Isaac. And thus, through all the generations of the righteous, as the muster-roll of the praying brotherhood increased, their argument was cumulative; till Christ summed it all up, for the future as well as for the past, in the one pregnant expression, " *Our* Father." Moreover, in this plurality there is embraced One who belongs to both the future and the past, and is the same yesterday, to-day, and for ever. So far as mere human fellowship is concerned, our prayers may be secret and solitary; but we can never pray entirely alone. A friend who sticketh closer than a brother is ever praying for us and with us. His intercessions are the much incense offered with the prayers of all saints upon the golden altar which is before the throne. " Go tell my brethren," says the risen Saviour in a message sent by Mary to his dispirited disciples, " I ascend unto my Father and your Father." *Yours* because he is *mine.* " I bow my knees," says Paul, " unto the Father of our Lord Jesus Christ, of whom the whole family in heaven and earth is named." Every child of that great family which bears his name recognizes not only the fatherhood of God, but also the brotherhood of Jesus Christ, which is properly included in it. The Teacher and the disciple, the Saviour and the sinner, have a blessed partnership at the mercy-seat. The need is all ours, and the merit all his. In the days of his flesh he offered up prayers and supplications with strong crying and tears. And now, though he has no need for himself, he continues to pray in our behalf. In view of his human yet divine fellowship with us, and his intercession for our sake, he taught his disciples this form of prayer. Therefore, when we pray, let us say not *my* Father, but *our* Father, in the full confidence that He is present and one with us.

III. Omnipresence is essential to the perfection of the divine nature. God is everywhere. He is before all things, in all, through all, over all, God blessed for evermore. Ubiquity is necessarily involved in his ability to hear prayer. This is one of those profound mysteries we can never solve, but which we are compelled to believe as the alternative of atheism. But God's omnipresence does not exclude the existence of one high and holy place, where he visibly reveals himself to angels and to the spirits of just men made perfect. That heaven, the abode of saints and angels, is literally a place, is easily demonstrated. A finite being must have some fixed relation to space. An angel or disembodied spirit cannot be everywhere. The Scriptures teach that they are all assembled in one place; beholding the face of our Father in heaven, worshipping God and the Lamb upon his throne, seeing him day without night in his temple. Moreover, the bodies of Enoch and Elijah, and the glorified humanity in which Christ ascended, must have some local habitation. In all the varied and splendid imagery employed in Scripture to describe the majesty of God and the blessed state of angels and glorified saints, a fixed abode is the central idea. Infinite space has abundant room, and the infinite God abundant resources for the fitting up of such an abode. On this subject the most literal is the most reasonable faith. The Saviour would have us thus believe when we approach our Father in prayer. He is everywhere, even here in our closet, where we pray in secret; and yet he is in heaven, and we are to direct our prayer to the place where his glory is openly revealed. It was so even under the more sensuous forms of the Old Dispensation. Solomon, standing by the altar of the temple built by God's own direction for his habitation, and before the holy place where the divine glory rested above the mercy-seat, said, "Hear thou *in heaven*, thy dwelling-place." Even the prophets of the circumcision exhorted, "Let us lift up our hearts with our hands unto God in the heavens." It is a good thing for the soul to be turned heavenward, saying, "I will direct my prayer unto thee, and will look up." That upward look to the things which are not seen and eternal is a blessed and life-giving exercise. Our carnal nature and this every-day world have enough to make us look down. We need constantly to be reminded, and to remind ourselves, that this spangled firmament and this green earth are not the whole of God's creation; nor this narrow life the only sphere in which we, children of immortality, are to have our being. And what is better fitted to exalt the soul from its earthliness than the habit of claiming kindred in prayer with One whose abode is far away beyond the stars, and whose life is not measured by the revolutions of these lower worlds?

The influence of thus praying to our Father *in heaven* extends further than this lifting up of the soul from things seen and temporal.

It derives precious lessons from all that we know of the character of heaven. Does our Father dwell in a place of infinite purity, into which nothing that worketh abomination or loveth a lie can ever enter? Do angels veil their faces before the brightness of his presence, and cry, "Holy, holy, holy is the Lord God Almighty"? How careful should we be, therefore, when we come to mingle our worship with the praises of that innumerable company, to lift up pure hands and a sincere heart before the throne! God is our Father, comes down *from* heaven to encourage our confidence; but still he is our Father *in* heaven. He claims our reverence as well as our confidence. We are not to talk to him as though he were a man, nor to take his glorious titles into our lips with a profane familiarity. "Be not rash with thy mouth, and let not thy heart be hasty to utter any thing before God: for God is in heaven, and thou upon earth; therefore let thy words be few."

And yet does he indeed stoop from his holy habitation and from the adoration of those perfect worshippers to listen to such prayers as ours? What infinite condescension is here! What pity in that eye which looks all the way from heaven to earth on the low estate of a sinful soul! What watchful care in that ear which, amid all the anthems of the skies, catches the whispered accents of the humblest disciple in his closet! What love in that infinite heart which says, "I dwell in the high and holy place, with him also who is of an humble and contrite spirit"! And how effectual must that love and pity be, since He who exercises them is seated on the throne which is established in heaven! We look up to that throne as to the hills whence cometh our strength. Our Father in heaven is but another name for our *Almighty* Father. And he that abideth under the shadow of the Almighty shall not be afraid.

Finally, if our Father is in heaven; if he makes that the place of his abode, and reveals himself there to the whole family that bears his name, — then heaven is our inheritance. If we are sons, then are we heirs, — heirs of God and joint-heirs with Jesus Christ. Where will our Father fix our permanent residence but in the place where his honor dwelleth? What will he bestow on his children, if not a permission to come home and share the abundance of his house? Let us cultivate a home feeling towards heaven. When we repeat the Lord's prayer, let it be a lesson to set our affections on things above, — a prophecy of our ingathering to the innumerable company of angels, and the general assembly of the church of the first-born which are written in heaven. In our Father's house are many mansions. There the excellent and lovely of all generations have entered into rest. There age delivered from its infirmities, and childhood set free from weakness and folly, are united in bonds of perfectness, and revel in pleasures for evermore. Every day adds to the number of that glorious and blessed household, and swells the tide of song in which the prayers of earth are turned into ecstatic praise. Child of God, can you think of the loving and the loved in your Father's house without longing to be there? Amid the sorrows of life, are you not sometimes homesick for heaven? How precious is the thought that He who taught us this prayer — before he ascended to his Father and our Father — promised to come again and receive us to himself, that where he is, there we may be also! O house of many mansions! O audience chamber of God our Father! O bright and transforming vision and fruition of Christ our Saviour! O sweet, perfect, eternal fellowship of angels and the spirits of just men made perfect! How dark and cold and fleeting, in comparison with you, are all the household joys and social bonds of this present evil world!

> "No shadows yonder!
>   All light and song:
> Each day I wonder,
>   And say, How long
> Shall time me sunder
>   From that blest throng?
>
> "No weeping yonder!
>   All fled away:
> While here I wander
>   Each weary day,
> And sigh as I ponder
>   My long, long stay.
>
> "No partings yonder!
>   Time and space never
> Again shall sunder:
>   Hearts cannot sever,
> Dearer and fonder
>   Hands clasp for ever."

CHAPTER II.

" Hallowed be Thy Name."

TRUE prayer is not the mere utterance of the lips, but the communion of the heart with God. And this communion is mutual; while we are speaking to him, his word, brought to remembrance by the indwelling spirit of truth, mingles frequent responses with our praises and petitions. Such responses from the divine oracle fill up and interpret every pause in the Lord's prayer. When we begin with the invocation, " Our Father which art in heaven," and stop a moment that our hearts may go up in concert with the full meaning of our words, do we not hear a voice from the excellent glory saying, " If I be a Father, where is my honor"? How searching and how humiliating is the question! We have not rendered to him the full honor which is his due. His pathetic complaint even in regard to his preferred people is, " Hear, O heavens, and be astonished, O earth. I have nourished and brought up children, and they have rebelled against me." It is a strange and unnatural thing that men should neglect the service and stand aloof from the fellowship of their Creator and Redeemer. It is still more strange that so many should regard the High and Holy One with hatred and aversion. But the strangest of all is, that we, who have received the spirit of adoption, should fall so often and so far below the apprehension of our privileges and the discharge of our corresponding obligations. And therefore, as the first commandment is, " Thou shalt have no other Gods before me," the first and great petition is, " Hallowed be thy name." It stands first not only in order, but in importance and perpetuity. Its spirit must overshadow and pervade the offering of all other petitions. We are to ask for daily bread, for the forgiveness of sins and deliverance from evil, only so far as these benefits are connected with the hallowing of our Father's name. And as this petition strikes the key-note of prayer on earth, it will constitute also the harmony of praise in heaven. In the home where there is no hunger, in the temple where there is no sin, in the paradise where the Old

Serpent cannot enter, the desire of all hearts and the utterances of all tongues will be concentrated in the hallowing of God's name.

The name of God, in the most obvious sense of the word, includes his peculiar titles. But as these titles are all divinely significant and true, his name is often spoken of as identical with his nature. Hence his titles are all holy even as he is holy. It is idolatry to give them to another; blasphemy to deny their appropriateness to him; profanity to repeat them without a profound reverence in the heart. And the same sacredness belongs to every thing he has chosen and sanctified for himself. His attributes, his word, and his ordinances are parts of his name. He is the God of the Bible, of the Sabbath, and of the sanctuary. In short, whatever is appropriated by him as a revelation of his character or an expression of his claims is to be hallowed, in proportion to the intimacy of the association and the fulness of the revelation. To hallow God's name, in the narrowest and most literal sense of the phrase, is to abstain from the profanation of every thing by which he is revealed to us. In this view, the petition before us is simply the third commandment turned into a prayer,—a prayer for deliverance from the sacrilege for which God will not hold men guiltless. But there is a more positive and a broader view. When an adopted son of God prays that his Father's name may be hallowed, his desires run parallel with those of the eternal Son when he cried, "Father, glorify thy name." We long with filial ardor to have the character of our heavenly Father more fully known and more adequately honored. We desire, and therefore we pray, that the number of his true worshippers may be increased, and that the reverence of all who approach his presence may be more sincere and fervent; that his glory may shine in the world and be duly acknowledged by all men, so that they may never think or speak of him without the deepest and holiest veneration; that all atheism, infidelity, superstition, and false religion may be banished from the world, and the only living and true God, our Father in heaven, be known, worshipped, and honored from the rising to the setting sun. Moreover, in the offering of such desires to God we consecrate ourselves to their consummation. It is not only a petition, but a vow; a solemn promise that by the grace we seek at his mercy-seat his name shall be hallowed in us.

The meaning of this part of the Lord's prayer may therefore be illustrated under a threefold division: the blessings we ask, the evil we deprecate, and the pledges we give.

I. The comprehensive blessing we ask is that God's glory may be more fully known and appreciated by us and by all men. That is but an earthly and sensual philosophy which exalts man as " the proper study of mankind." And its infidel spirit is but poorly concealed under the pretence that it is presumptuous to scan the being and character of God. The desire and search of the finite soul after the infinite one, of the mortal after the immortal, of the creature in his conscious weakness and dependence after the supreme and all-sufficient Creator, of the sinner in a world of sin and sorrow after a divine Redeemer, is the highest and best instinct of our nature. It is the grand distinction between an immortal man and a beast that perishes. It is written on every page of the Bible; and for those who read in its light the divine handiwork of the heaven and the earth, or study under its guidance the testimony of man's consciousness, it is written on the face of nature and on the human heart that the proper study of mankind is GOD. When the morning stars sang together, the glory of the Creator was their theme; and the same theme is the fundamental note of that unceasing symphony in which day unto day uttereth speech and night unto night showeth knowledge. "Acquaint thyself with him, and be at peace," is the voice of experience from the history of the first patriarch. "To know him aright is life eternal" is the response of the last apostle. "God had no rest from the creation till he had made man, and man can have no rest in the creation till he rests in God. The human spirit never rises to its original glory till carried up on the wings of faith and love to its original copy."* The Bible sums up the perfections of God in three brief sentences, whose depth of meaning no finite line can fathom: *God is a spirit, God is light, God is love!* Oh could we grasp and imbue our being with the full meaning of these pregnant statements our spirits would rise and expand into the likeness of the Father of spirits, our whole body would be full of light, our whole soul would be purified and kindled into holy joy by the power of infinite and eternal love! The perfection of such knowledge is too wonderful for us: it is high, we cannot

* Charnock.

attain to it. And yet, if we are God's children and have a covenant right to call him our Father, he "has shined into our hearts to give us the light of the knowledge of his glory in the face of Jesus Christ." We have attained to some right, though inadequate, apprehensions of the infinite, eternal, and unchangeable spirit; have caught some gleamings from that inaccessible fountain of light, and felt to a blessed, though imperfect, degree the plastic power of that eternal love. And because we have thus been with God on the mount of communion, we cry out with the leader of Israel, "I beseech thee show me thy glory." Let me see thee, not as hitherto through a glass darkly, but face to face. Let me know and feel, at least for one ecstatic moment, the full reality and grandeur of thy existence and perfections. Such desires are no disparagement to the completeness and sufficiency of divine revelation. They contemplate only the fulfilment of what is written: the quickening of the dead letter into spirit and into life, so that the revelation on the sacred page may be transferred with divine power to the heart; the full accomplishment of the end for which revelation was given, so that "all men may see what is the fellowship of the mystery which from the beginning of the world hath been hid in God." To see God is the final and complete beatitude of the pure in heart. To have all men see and acknowledge his glory, even though they refuse his dominion, is the loving and loyal ambition of every true child of our Father in heaven. How beautifully is this filial spirit illustrated by the Saviour, when even in the hour and power of darkness, though his soul was troubled, he cried, "Father, glorify thy name"! Then came there a voice from heaven, saying, "I have both glorified it and will glorify it again." This promise is the ground and plea of faith. The great mystery of time, and the great trial of faith, is the long delay in its fulfilment. God seems to withdraw from the visible control of the world, and hide himself from the searchings of his people. Meantime, his name is profaned and his honor trampled in the dust. His authority is disputed, and his very existence is denied. The philosopher and the fool combine in this crusade of atheism. The one arrays the divine order and beauty of the things which are made against the very being of the Creator: the other drowns all thought of things unseen and eternal in the enjoyments of sense; and both set their mouths against the heavens, saying, "Where is the promise of his coming? for since the fathers fell asleep all things continue as they were." "Therefore his people return hither, and the waters of a full cup are wrung out to them." And the bitterest ingredients in that full cup are the atheistic doubts which cause us to cry now and again, "Where is God my maker? O that I knew where I might find him. Behold I go forward, but he is not there; and backward, but I cannot perceive him; on the left hand where he doth work, but I cannot behold him: he hideth himself on the right hand that I cannot see him." From the principalities and powers of spiritual wickedness, whether arrayed under the banner of carnal sense or the more subtle leadership of the Positive philosophy, the only sure refuge is the mercy-seat. We must "wrestle" with these powers of darkness before the throne. It is in vain for a child of God to fight this battle in his own strength or with weapons drawn from the armory of reason. Let him imbibe the spirit and appropriate the words of Christ, "Father, glorify thy name." "O Shepherd of Israel, thou that dwellest between the cherubim, shine forth ; that all the people of the earth may know thy name to fear thee. How long, O Lord, wilt thou hide thyself? O God, how long shall the adversary reproach? Shall the enemy blaspheme thy name for ever? Why withdrawest thou thy right hand? Pluck it out of thy bosom. Put them in fear, O Lord, that the nations may know themselves to be but men." Come down upon this blaspheming and apostate earth, as thou didst on Mount Sinai of old, that all the people may tremble and bow down at the proclamation of thy great name, and that thy servants may know of a surety that thou art the ever living and true God. So let thy name be HALLOWED.

II. But while the petition has this broad meaning and contemplates a fuller revelation of the divine glory to us and to all men, it has also a more intimate and personal significance. To us, and to those with whom we pray, God has revealed himself in his works, his word, his providence, and by his spirit. We cannot offer this prayer without a humiliating sense of our failure to glorify him as God to the extent of our knowledge. And therefore, with a penitent review of the past as well as a hopeful glance at the future, we deprecate the sins which are peculiarly dishonoring to his name.

1. We deprecate all false and unscriptural thoughts of God.

Right views of the divine attributes are the foundation of all sound theology. Tell me what view a man takes of the divine attributes, and I will rehearse to you all his creed. The Bible doctrine of sin and its punishment is the outgrowth of God's holiness. The sacrifice of the cross is inseparably connected with his justice no less than with his love. Providence is but the exercise of his omnipresence and omniscience, his wisdom and his power; and the whole scheme of divine foreordination is linked by an inexorable logic with the simple recognition of his foreknowledge and sovereignty. And so, also, all heresy runs back into the denial or obscuration of the divine perfections. The advocates of error always pretend to be very zealous for the vindication of the divine honor; but while they give a distorted and unscriptural exhibition of some one of God's attributes, they invariably ignore and deny the qualities which he most frequently and explicitly claims for himself. So far is it from being a matter of indifference what we think about God, that the thought of our heart concerning him is the index and measure of both our creed and our moral character. The counsel of the ungodly is the first step towards the seat of the scorner. The great charge against apostate men is, "Thou thoughtest I was altogether such an one as thyself." And whether it be carried out to the making of an image like corruptible man, or only cherished in the heart as a prejudgment of the doctrines of revelation, this thought of the heart is itself the very essence of idolatry. Men strip Jehovah of the attributes which are essential to his great name, persuade themselves that he is just what they would like him to be; and thus set up an idol, which is no more like the God of the Bible than is the carved image on a Hindoo shrine.

2. Hence, also, in this petition we deprecate all deceitful handling of the word of God. Here he has recorded the precious thoughts which are above our thoughts, and answered the great question, "What is truth?" Here, in the person and life of the incarnate Word, he has responded to the desire of the human heart to see God. "He that hath seen me

hath seen the Father; and how sayest thou then, Shew us the Father?" Here is his great name written in characters so large and luminous that a child's eye may read it. Well may we pray to be delivered from the blindness of the pretended philosopher, who professes to trace God's footprints in his works, and yet cannot see his glorious face in the pages his breath has inspired; and no less from the infidelity of the false prophet, who blots and tears the sacred record to wrest it to the support of the doctrines and commandments of men. God's Book is perfect as a whole and in all its parts. His image and superscription are on every chapter. As when the brightness of the sun, breaking out of showers, shines on the smallest raindrop that hangs upon a leaf no less than on the broad river spread out like a sheet of burnished gold; so God's name shines in every part and particle of these sacred pages. If we would hallow that name we must hide this word in our hearts. We must receive it in its rigid exclusiveness as *the* truth. If we find here some hard doctrine, some fearful exhibition of divine holiness and justice, we must not cavil and find fault. The child that invokes the blessing of "our

Father" must say, with little Samuel, " Speak, Lord, thy servant heareth." We must not whittle away the plain meaning of God's word to make the sense square with our notions. May he keep us from such unhallowed pride. And so also may he deliver us from the irreverence that makes a jest book, a conjurer's book, or a vain ornament out of the Bible! If we would hallow his name we must not play upon the words in which it is revealed; neither must we mutter these sacred words as though they were a heathen charm to exorcise evil, aside from their intelligent application to our understanding; nor cut these holy pages to tell our fortune as with a pack of cards; nor set them up, gilded and embossed on the outside, as a household idol, under the vain notion that we honor God's word by making it a decoration in the drawing-room, instead of taking it into our closet as the man of our counsel and the guide of our life.

3. Moreover, in this petition we deprecate all profaning of God's ordinances. His first ordinance is the Sabbath: first in time, for it dates back to the finishing of creation and the innocence of Paradise; first also in impor-

tance, for it underlies and upholds all the institutions of divine worship. It is identified with the history and progress of religion; and never did any man or people hallow his name without honoring his day and calling it a delight. Search the Scriptures, and see what curses are denounced against those who profane the Sabbath, what blessings are heaped up upon those who sanctifiy it from worldly business and pleasure. See, too, in the history of individuals, how Sabbath-breaking not only shuts a man out from the means of grace, but hardens his heart against God, and makes him reprobate concerning every good work. A Sabbath-breaker is always and necessarily a profane man in other respects. The beginning of his sin is a disregard for God's holiness and authority, and by its habitual commission he must increase unto more ungodliness.

So also in regard to all the ordinances of worship. God says, "I will be sanctified in them that come near me." Holy angels approach his presence with veiled faces and hearts full of worship, and words of adoration on their lips. And " shall men rush in where angels fear to tread?" Nay, "keep thy foot when thou goest to the house of God; and be more ready to hear than to give the sacrifice of fools." Church-going is not a mere matter of taste or recreation. It is solemn business transacted with God for eternity. If we enter God's house out of a mere regard for this or that man, to indulge our love of music or eloquence, to gratify our curiosity, or to make a vain display, our presence is an offence in his sight. "It is iniquity, even the solemn meeting." Surely we have need in these Athenian days to pray for deliverance from the sin of a careless, formal, and man-honoring worship. May "our Father" help his ministers to exalt and honor him; and give the people grace to say in every assembly, "Now, then, we are all here present before God, to hear all things that are commanded thee of God."

4. Furthermore, in this petition we deprecate all profane use of God's titles and attributes.

It is among the dishonors the world puts upon our Maker, to magnify the second table of the law above the first. Because murder and theft and adultery and slander are crimes committed directly against human society, and touch us in our persons and our property, we regard them as the greatest sins; while at the same time we think it is comparatively a small thing to steal God's honor, and assault his person, and trample his glory in the dust. We overlook the significance of the fact that when he came down on Sinai to proclaim his law, next to his claim to exclusive worship he thundered forth the command, "Thou shalt not take the name of the Lord thy God in vain." The violation of this command is one of the great sins of the world, whether we consider its prevalence, its influence, or its intrinsic enormity. For its prevalence, it pollutes the atmosphere of society; it comes up, like the vermin plagues of Egypt, into the palace and the cottage; it invades the senate-chamber and the court-room, and taints the fountains of public justice; it runs riot unrebuked in our streets, and dances in our gay assemblies, and crawls into our nurseries to blast the budding piety of our children, and rises black and foul, like the smoke of the pit, to envelop our theatres and dram-shops, and all the open gateways to perdition. As to its influence and its enormity, in all its forms,—from the perjury of the false witness down through all its gradations to the sweetened and diluted blasphemy that sports on the lips of a gay lady, — it is the distilled essence of sin, the fumes of corruption in a heart at enmity with God. There is no sense, nor good breeding, nor manhood in it. It cannot be palliated by the craving of any natural appetite, save only the love of sin. It brings with it no gratification, except the satanic pleasure of defiling the name all heaven delights to honor.

> "Take not his name, who made thy mouth, in vain!
> It gets thee nothing, and has no excuse.
> Lust and wine plead a pleasure, avarice gain;
> But the cheap swearer, through his open sluice,
> Lets his soul run for naught."

God keep us from profanity that we may hallow his name.

III. In the offering of this petition, as indeed in all our prayers, we give pledges to God that our efforts will be in the line of our supplications. The double-minded and unstable man need not expect to receive any thing of the Lord. The hearer of the word who is not also a doer of the work only mocks God with his prayers. True reverence for his name is doubtless a fruit of the Holy Spirit,

THE MODEL PRAYER. 49

and we are to ask for it as a divine gift. But the reception of any such gift involves co-operation on our part. We are to work out what he works in us. If therefore we would hallow God's name, we must strive to realize by experience what is meant by being sober-minded. Sobriety is not synonymous, neither has it any necessary connection, with sadness or gloom. It means simply that integrity of mind and heart which treats all subjects in a manner suitable to their own character. We may trifle with trifles; we may laugh at that which is laughable. Though we are to give an account for every idle word, it does not follow that every idle word will condemn us. But God and the human soul, heaven and hell, sin and salvation, are all serious subjects, and can never be made a theme for merriment without a violation of sobriety amounting to guilt. There is no amusement in the conversion or damnation of men. "Fools make a mock of sin;" and the irreverence which mingles sacred things with "jestings which are not convenient" is no better than the crackling of thorns in the fire that consumes them.

Intimately connected with sobriety of mind

is the government of the tongue. Words are things. They not only indicate the fulness of the heart, but react upon it, and intensify its prevailing temper. The tongue defileth the whole body. Let us beware of the first kindling of this fire. Small oaths are the seeds of great ones. The profane use of God's attributes; the habit of searching the Scriptures not for eternal life, but to find jests, to pander to prurient passions, or to find cavils against the truth; the idle gossip about ministers and churches; and the shallow, flippant discussion of holy things which dissipates serious impressions, — are all sparks from below with which Satan is ever ready to set on fire the course of nature. As we govern ourselves in regard to these things, so ought we, to the extent of our authority, to govern those who are under our control. Let us stand up on all suitable occasions for the honor of our Father in heaven; and especially, if we are at the head of a family, let us " command our children and our household after us to keep the ways of the Lord." Sabbath-breaking and profanity should not be permitted in a Christian family. Books full of infidelity and blasphemy, — of making which, alas! there is no end, — when

THE MODEL PRAYER. 51

they creep into the sacred circle of home like the Serpent into Paradise, ought to be purified in the fire and buried in the ashes. If higher motives fail, the rod of correction should drive profanity from the lips of a child. And, in the case of servants and grown-up children, an outward respect for God's holy name ought to be enforced at the risk of banishment. These are old-fashioned notions, but none the less precious on that account; for they are the teachings of Scripture sanctified and embalmed in the experience of God's people in every age.

Finally, if we would hallow God's name and vindicate our sincerity in the offering of this prayer, we must acquire for ourselves and cherish as our chief treasure an intimate knowledge of the holy Scriptures. Here only we can learn what God is and what he requires. He has magnified his word above all his name. Filling our heart and lips with these revelations of truth, and our imaginations with these inspired images of holiness, we shall be meet for the fellowship of those who pay all honor and present a perfect worship to " the King eternal, immortal, and invisible, the only wise God our Saviour." Few of us are aware how precious God's revealed thoughts are to us in their silent, all-pervading influence; how much we owe to the Scriptures not only for the knowledge of our Father's character, but for every sentiment and affection that assimilates us to him, or fits us for the fellowship of the wise and the holy in his service. It is the most blessed feature of the minister's office, that it is a stewardship of the mysteries of God, and therefore a ministry of the word in which those mysteries are revealed. It is the consecration of a life to the study and exposition of the Bible. It brings the heart and mind into daily contact with the divine beauty, vitality, and power of that one book, which is not only the revelation of God's will, but the transcript of his character. It leads the thirsty soul to drink not at human reservoirs fetid with stagnant waters, but at pure and abundant streams flowing from the heart of God. And thus the very work of the ministry becomes its own exceeding great reward. No true preacher of God's word would exchange, for all the wealth of the world, the treasures with which that word has enriched his own mind, the sense of the glory of the divine being with which it has suffused his soul, and the ecstatic reverence for God's name, which is the earnest of beholding his face in righteousness and being satisfied with his likeness. Nor is such experience confined to ministers and professed expounders of the Scriptures. Why should it be? God's word is the heritage, the treasure-house, the fountain of living waters of all his children. Its entrance gives light to the most obscure, and elevates the most lowly to a true spiritual refinement. As the little flower that drinks in unconsciously the ethereal mildness and glory of the spring feels the power of these celestial influences no less than the cedar of Lebanon, the humblest Christian who writes God's word upon the door-posts of his house and of his heart, interweaves it with his experience, and makes it familiar to his soul as the air and the light to his senses, will become all glorious within; his raiment will be of wrought gold, and all his garments will smell of myrrh and aloes and cassia out of the ivory palace. And thus while he hallows his heavenly Father's name, he will himself be hallowed by it; while he glorifies God, his own soul will be glorified by the assimilating power of that divine word, which, amid the human glories that wither and fade like the flower of the grass, liveth and abideth for ever. For

> " The law of the Lord is perfect,
> Converting the soul :
> The testimony of the Lord is sure,
> Making wise the simple :
> The statutes of the Lord are right,
> Rejoicing the heart :
> The commandment of the Lord is pure,
> Enlightening the eyes :
> The fear of the Lord is clean,
> Enduring for ever :
> The judgments of the Lord are true
> And righteous altogether :
> More to be desired are they than gold,
> Yea than much fine gold :
> Sweeter also than honey,
> And the honey-comb."

CHAPTER III.

" Thy Kingdom come."

THE comprehensiveness of the Lord's prayer, wonderful in reference to the other Scriptures, is no less so in regard to itself. When we consider it collectively, it appears to be an epitome of all revealed truth. When we meditate on its separate sentences, it seems to fold itself up into a still smaller compass, — each part presenting an abridgment of the whole, and every petition embracing the substance of all prayer. Thus the first petition limits and interprets all the rest; for we ought not to desire pardon or deliverance from sin, or even our daily bread, except so far as they are consistent with the hallowing of God's name. Especially does this first petition overlap and interpenetrate the two following; and the three together, like the first table of the Law, sum up the claims of God's honor and glory. The hallowing of his name involves the coming of his kingdom; and the coming of his kingdom both pre-supposes and secures the doing of his will on earth as it is in heaven.

"The beginning of the work of God in us is the hallowing of his name: the form in which the divine work is perfected, as well as the means by which it comes to perfection, is the kingdom of God. This kingdom was prefigured in Israel: it was introduced in its essence by Christ; and through his power it advances ever more and more in the course of the ages towards its perfection. Thus the second petition, 'thy kingdom come,' is connected with the first, and again with the third, which indicates the final goal and end of all things, the removal of all distraction, and the perfect harmony of the creature with the will of the Creator. These three petitions accordingly present to us the beginning, middle, and end of the development of the kingdom of God." *

I. The Scriptures speak of the kingdom of God in a fourfold sense: 1. The KINGDOM of his POWER, or his universal providence over all the works of his hands. In this sense "the Lord hath prepared his throne in the heavens, and his

* Tholuck.

dominion ruleth over all." 2. The KINGDOM of the GOSPEL, or the New Testament dispensation, as the forerunner of which John the Baptist cried, "Repent, for the kingdom of heaven is at hand." 3. The KINGDOM of GRACE, or the dominion of God in the hearts of regenerate men. This is the kingdom which is *within* you, which " is righteousness and peace, and joy in the Holy Ghost." 4. The KINGDOM of GLORY, or the everlasting blessedness of the saints, which is prepared for them before the foundation of the world, and which Christ will welcome them to inherit in the last great day.

To the first of these, it is evident that the petition before us does not refer. God's dominion over all his works cannot *come*. It was in the beginning, is now, and ever shall be perfect and entire. He is God over all, blessed for evermore. It is only so far as we are fully persuaded of his absolute and eternal dominion that we can have any intelligent encouragement to pray; and therefore, in token not only of our desire, but our expectation, to be heard, we conclude our petitions with the sublime doxology, " thine *is* the kingdom, and the power, and the glory for ever. *Amen.*"

It is further evident that the three remaining senses of the phrase "kingdom of God" refer to different aspects of the same thing. The kingdom of the gospel, the kingdom of grace, and the kingdom of glory are only successive stages in the development of that one scheme by which God designs to overrule the apostasy of men and of angels, for his own glory and the good of his chosen people. It is for the full consummation and triumph of the great plan of redemption, — whether in the outward dispensation of the gospel, the inward dominion of grace in the heart, or the final development of grace into the glory of heaven, — that we pray in the petition " thy kingdom come."

We pray that the Christian dispensation may be diffused over the whole earth, that the gospel may be preached for a witness among all nations and to every creature ; because we know that, without the knowledge of the gospel, there is no salvation. "For whosoever shall call on the name of the Lord shall be saved. How, then, shall they call on him in whom they have not believed? And how shall they believe in him of whom they have not heard? And how shall they hear without a preacher?" And we know also that there is no salvation, even with the knowledge of the gospel, unless it be accompanied and made effectual by a divine power which God only can exercise.

And therefore we pray that the kingdom of grace may come in the hearts of men. The conversion of a soul to God may well be compared to the setting up of a kingdom. It is a conquest, and a triumph, a revolution, and the birth of an empire. Old things have passed away, and all things have become new. There is a new allegiance, new affections, new desires and objects of pursuit. Other Lords have had dominion over us; but now grace rules both the understanding and the heart, and brings the whole man into subjection to Christ. Loyalty to his crown and kingdom is now the master passion of the soul. Every heart in which that kingdom is set up " indites a good matter," and makes " the tongue the pen of a ready writer." And this is the fair song which the heart welleth forth: —

> " Thou art fairer than the children of men:
> Grace is poured into thy lips:
> Therefore God hath blessed thee for ever.
> Gird thy sword upon thy thigh,
> O most mighty,
> With thy glory and thy majesty;

> And in thy majesty ride prosperously
> Because of truth and meekness and righteousness;
> And thy right hand shall teach thee terrible things."
>
> *Psalm* xlv.

Every one translated from the power of darkness to the kingdom of God's dear Son indites such good matter, not only for himself, but for others. He would have his relatives and friends converted to God. He would witness and rejoice in the triumphs of his Father's grace in his own neighborhood and country. He longs for the time when the King he adores shall ride prosperously through every land. In such desires all the children of God are one, and the great Teacher only interprets the hearts of his disciples when he instructs us to pray " thy kingdom come."

But the kingdom of grace, great and blessed as it is, is not perfect nor final. It is but the earthly bud of an immortal flower, — the porch of that temple where they need no candle, neither light of the sun, — the morning twilight of a heavenly and perfect day. If we use this petition intelligently, we pray for the consummation of grace in the kingdom of glory. No true child of God desires to live alway. " Let them fear death who do not fear sin; but let not God's children be overmuch troubled at the grim face of that messenger which brings them to the end of their sorrow, and the completion of their joy."*

This world is no satisfying portion, no abiding home for us. There are too many vacant places in the circle of its friendship, too many bitter memories that time cannot efface, too many infirmities in the body, and too many imperfections in the soul. In this house we groan, being burdened. And, on the other hand, the love is too pure, the repose too sweet, the joy too ecstatic, the glory too infinite and eternal, in yonder city of our God, for us to find any continuing city here. When animal instincts and earthly affections have the upper hand, when we labor for the bread that perishes and are absorbed by things seen and temporal, it may seem desirable that our days on earth should be stretched out to the utmost limit. But when the instincts of our new natures have full sway, and we look up to the things not seen and eternal, and consider the ties which bind us to the everlasting kingdom of God, it seems " better to depart; " and we are ready to cry, " Come, Lord Jesus ! Come quickly ! "

* Thomas Watson.

When the soul is filled with such desires for ourselves they overflow upon others. Selfish affection may cling to living friends, and selfish grief mourn over those who sleep in Jesus; but no true child of God would so curse his brother as to say to him, "Live for ever." For the same reason that we would have our friends converted, our heart consents to their full redemption and their passing away, in God's good time, into the kingdom of glory.

Moreover, the same sentiments apply to the termination of the present probationary state of the world, and the introduction of that glorious period when the kingdom of grace shall be co-extensive with the gospel dispensation, and both shall cover and pervade the earth. The kingdom of God has been the scene of many marvellous events. The incarnation and ministry of Christ, and the successes of his apostles, were one continuous miracle. But the sure word of prophecy assures us that we shall "see greater things than these." God's kingdom is still in its infancy. Its chief glory is yet to be developed and revealed. The stone cut out without hands from the mountain shall smite and break in pieces and consume the image of all secular power; and the greatness of the kingdom under the whole heavens shall be given to the saints of the Most High, and all dominions shall serve him. (Dan. ii. 45, vii. 27.) Evil shall be banished, and truth shall triumph in the earth. Yea, there shall be a new heaven and a new earth wherein dwelleth righteousness. The glowing and varied descriptions of the kingdom of God, in its ultimate development and triumph, found in the Old Testament Scriptures and erroneously applied by Jewish expounders to the first coming of Christ, are repeated in the New Testament in connection with "the glorious hope" of his second advent. The reappearance of our ascended Lord in the clouds of heaven, in the glory of the Father, and with all the holy angels, is the leading and crowning event of all those scenes amid which the gospel dispensation shall fade and be absorbed into the everlasting light and blessedness of heaven. This is the promise for which the primitive disciples watched and waited with joyful anticipations. Their interest was not absorbed nor their efforts expended in the rise or fall of human empires, which are all destined to be destroyed, but in the final coming of that kingdom, which, though it is not of this world in its origin or its elements, will nevertheless subject this world to its control. Oh for the revival of that primitive and exclusive faith! Amid the changes and corruptions of human governments, and the conflicts of temporal power, how few, even of God's people, remember as they should their fellow-citizenship with the saints, and wait for their Lord at his coming! The secularization of the church for ages has clouded her vision, and relaxed the sinews of her strength. Even among those who look most ardently for the second advent of our Saviour King, the subject has passed too much out of the atmosphere of the mercy-seat into the cold and misty region of theological speculation. There is too little prayer for his coming, and too much effort to demonstrate *when* and *how* he will come. The revival of the primitive faith on this subject does not render it necessary to settle, or even to consider, all the disputes in regard to it. Whether Christ's advent will be *pre*, or *post* millennial; whether he will come in visible splendor *before* the final triumph of the gospel, and in order to usher in its ultimate success, or whether he will delay his coming till *after* that success has been achieved through his promised blessing on human agencies; when, and at what precise point in the winding up of this dispensation, the resurrection and the general judgment will take place, and in what particular order they will be conducted; whether this earth, renovated and made part of heaven, or some new region far away beyond the stars, will be the everlasting dwelling-place of the blessed;— these and many more such questions are altogether aside from the simple, sublime, glorious hope that Christ will come again in the glory of the Father, that the gospel will triumph, that the saints of God from all ages will be gathered into one kingdom and made perfectly blessed in the enjoyment of himself for ever! The difficulty of deciding such questions, and the presumption of some who have undertaken by expounding the prophecies to make themselves prophets, should not be suffered to discredit the promise, or darken in any believing soul the great hope of the New Dispensation. The times and the seasons, which it is not for us to know, should be no hindrance to our faith in the revealed things which belong to us and to our children.

II. The reasons which should urge us to pray for the coming of God's kingdom, in all its phases and through all the stages of its predicted triumphs, are unspeakably weighty and urgent.

God's kingdom is founded in righteousness. How different in this respect from the kingdoms of this world, whose history is, for the most part, a record of usurpation and crime! There is not an earthly throne which has not been baptized in blood; nor a royal family whose power and riches have not been built up by gigantic wrongs; nor a human government which does not contain the seeds of corruption and decay. But God's right to reign is perfect and eternal. Justice and judgment are the habitation of his throne. And when we add to this natural and inherent right the consideration of his infinite fitness to reign, every sentiment of truth and honor should impel us to desire and pray that his kingdom may come.

The complete coming of God's kingdom will remove all the evils that afflict the world. It will destroy the works of the devil, overthrow the powers of darkness, cast out the Prince of this world from his usurped domin-

THE MODEL PRAYER.

ion, and bind Satan, the great adversary of God and men, in everlasting chains. The existence of this great adversary and the reality of his spiritual dominion are revealed in the Scriptures just as plainly as the being of God. It was no abstract personification of wickedness that assailed Christ in the wilderness; still less was it any struggling of evil passions in his own heart that tempted Him who knew no sin, during those forty days and nights. Such interpretations are blasphemous. The tempter is a real being, a mighty apostate from God, worshipped and followed by an innumerable host of fallen spirits, and struggling from age to age for the dominion of the world. He rules in the hearts of the children of disobedience. With a force and subtlety none but God can overmatch, he resists the progress of the gospel, fights against the dominion of grace in the soul, and struggles to prevent the coming of the kingdom of glory. With this empire of Satan the crimes and miseries of the world are inseparably connected: they can never cease till that empire is destroyed, and this apostate world brought back to its allegiance to God. The weapons by which this triumph is to be achieved are not carnal, but spiritual. The great disease of humanity is sin: the only infallible remedy is salvation. The bitter fountain of all evil is the alienation of men from God, and their confederation with the spirit of disobedience: the only deliverance from evil is the coming of that kingdom which is not of this world. The tyrants who desolate the earth, and shut the gates of mercy on mankind, can never be dispossessed of their usurped dominion, till the King eternal, immortal, and invisible is fully honored as our Father. Till then human revolutions are but a change of masters; and human reformations only the damming up of the waters of sin for a time, to break out again with accumulated violence. Even the governments that are professedly based on the recognition of human rights are built on the sand; because they assume, in the face of the divine testimony and of experience, that the people for whose benefit they are established are, and will continue to be, intelligent and virtuous: an assumption which has never been justified in the history of the world, and never can be true, until God's rights are recognized as supreme, and God's law accepted as the universal rule of life.

THE MODEL PRAYER.

The Utopian dream of political and social perfectibility, aside from the conversion of men to God through the power of the gospel; the hope of a kingdom founded in right, and administered in justice, and destined to perpetuity, has thrown its fascinations over the minds of men from the beginning of the world; and still, after a thousand failures, each new experiment holds out the same deceitful promise, and too often enlists the enthusiasm even of Christ's professed disciples. Oh that God's people would remember that he has given the kingdoms of this world to our Lord, not that he may conserve and perpetuate them, and chain his glory to their chariot-wheels, and mingle his triumphs with their blood-stained victories; but that he may "break them with a rod of iron, and dash them in pieces as a potter's vessel." (Ps. ii.) Let those who have sworn allegiance to the crown of Christ cease from the hero-worship of the world; and, leaving the potsherd to strive with the potsherds of the earth, let them pray and wait for the coming of that kingdom which cannot be moved. For in it are centred all our hopes for suffering humanity, all our earnest expectation that the groaning and travailing together of creation will come to an end, all our visions of established peace on earth and good-will toward men. And with the same consummation the accomplishment of our personal destiny as the adopted children of God is identified. Till that kingdom comes *within* us, in the fulness of its righteousness and peace and joy in the Holy Ghost, our own true character will not attain its perfect development. Till that kingdom comes around us, in the revealed power and glory of him we serve, our true position in the universe can neither be recognized by others nor fully realized by ourselves. "For it doth not yet appear what we shall be; but we know that when he shall appear we shall be like *him*." Some there are who dig among the rubbish of the world's departed glory, as though every thing to be desired were buried with the cities whose memorials have perished with them; and some are absorbed and smitten with admiration for the age that now is, claiming for the present generation a pre-eminence in terrestrial glory. But, Christians, your glory is celestial, and lies in the future. All the past and all the present are tributary to it, even as all rivers flow into the sea. The memorials of the kingdom to which you belong do not perish; they are laid up on high. Others may be sons of princes; but you are sons of God. You belong to the primogeniture of heaven. Patriarchs, prophets, and apostles are your kinsmen. Saints chosen and called out of every age and land, witnesses for the truth of whom the world was not worthy, are fellow-citizens with you. Ye are a chosen generation, a royal priesthood, a holy nation, a peculiar people called out of darkness into marvellous light. Your individual destiny is bound up with the kingdom of God. As the night-watch anticipates the morning, as the heir looks forward to his inheritance, so look and long for the day-dawn of heaven on earth, and for the glory which is to be revealed in you. While others hail the coming *man*, watch and wait for your returning Lord. And while the shadows of this night of weeping still linger around the portals of the sky, let your hearts' desire and prayer to God be, " Thy kingdom come."

III. As the promises were not given to supersede, but to quicken and encourage prayer, so in its turn prayer is appointed not merely to express desire, but to stimulate effort. Without works, the faith it embodies is dead. He that says sincerely, "Thy kingdom come," will often speak of that kingdom out of the fulness of his heart. His thoughts will be more absorbed in the progress of the gospel and the conversion of men than in the politics or business of the world. And his supreme interest will be manifest not in words only, but in corresponding deeds. He will make personal efforts to bring men under the dominion of Christ. He will take large and liberal views of the Christian enterprises whose weapon is the gospel and whose end is to conquer the world for Christ. He will not be offended when asked to contribute means for their support. He will consider it a privilege to give, — to lay up his treasures where his heart is also. Such a man will train his family to the same liberal views. He will desire that his daughters may be "all glorious within," so that the King may "greatly desire their beauty." He will teach his sons that the great business of life is not to heap up riches on earth, but to become rich towards God; and if the Lord of the harvest shall call them into the ministry, he will feel that his blood is ennobled by flowing in the veins of those who are standard-bearers in the kingdom of God.

How gross is the inconsistency, when those who pray, "Thy kingdom come," show by the spirit of their whole life that they are interested in any thing rather than the propagation of the gospel, and are more ready to invest their efforts and riches in worldly than in Christian enterprises! Viewed in this light, the whole Christian Church stands in a most humiliating attitude before God and the world. The aggregate of her labors and gifts for the upbuilding of Christ's kingdom are in painful contrast with the more liberal devotion which, as children of this world, her professed adherents prosecute their schemes for the acquisition of temporal power and riches.

These things ought not so to be. It was not so in the beginning. After the great outpouring of the Holy Spirit on the day of Pentecost, "the multitude that believed were of one heart and one soul; neither said any of them that aught of the things which he possessed was his own." These primitive disciples understood the great doctrine of stewardship to God. They were ready to invest their all in the great Christian enterprise, with greater ardor than the men of the world embark in commercial speculations. And the result was, that more was done to advance the gospel in the first century than has been accomplished in the eighteen that have followed. So it will be again, when the church is baptized anew with the Holy Ghost as with fire, and all her members regard themselves as stewards of God, and servants of his kingdom. They must have a low estimate of Christ's claims upon his blood-bought people, and a very imperfect apprehension of apostolic example, who think that the church in this or any other land has come up to the standard of her destiny and her duty. The great revival is yet to be experienced. The Protestant Reformation, and the triumphs of the Pentecost, and the conquering zeal of primitive Christianity, are all to be thrown into the shade by the dawning of a more glorious day. It is not enough to pray, " Thy kingdom come." The voice of God answers again from heaven, — while the Red Sea bars the way before, and the hosts of Egypt press on behind, — saying, " Wherefore criest thou unto me? speak unto the children of Israel that they go forward." Blessed are the eyes that see the triumph from afar, and the ears that catch the shout of victory from beyond the flood, and the hearts that are kindled by the enthusiasm of the coming glory!

We live in an age which builds monuments of science and civilization more magnificent than the pyramids. Mountains and oceans interposed are no barriers to the swift thoughts and purposes of men. An intense life pervades the nations. Commerce with its quick instincts is breaking through all obstructions, building its highways over sea and land, and erecting its storehouses in every clime. Human thought is pushing its investigations into the bowels of the earth and far away among the orbits of the stars, and weaving its theories in every direction. It remains for those who profess Christ's name, and especially for those to whom he has given largely of the abundance of the earth, to determine whether the outward triumphs of civilization shall be consecrated to God or to the devil; whether the gross materialism, under which the great empires of antiquity rotted at the core and crumbled into decay, shall pervade the progress of modern times, and prepare the way for a new inroad of barbarism; whether papal superstition shall succeed in its desperate efforts to adapt itself to the changed circumstances of the world, and darken the ages to come as it has darkened the ages that are past; or whether now, after so long a time, the light of the pure gospel shall shine on unclouded, till earth and heaven shall together renew the prophetic cry, "Babylon is fallen, and the kingdom of heaven is at hand!" Let us not be deceived: mere civilization can never secure permanent peace and prosperity, even in this world; especially when it decks the bride of Christ in the attire of a harlot, and makes her heart gross with the thought that gain is godliness.

But oh! if the science that is spanning continents with cunning fingers, and traversing oceans in its giant strides, might be imbued with the spirit of Christ, and the treasures that are poured into the lap of commerce might be consecrated to the preaching of the gospel; these eyes that have grown dim with watching for the morning may yet behold the latter day glory; and these lips and hearts, long burdened with prayer for its coming, may take up the song of praise, "Glory to God! thy kingdom *has* come."

CHAPTER IV.

"Thy Will be done in Earth as it is in Heaven."

A TRULY devout soul loves to contemplate the blessedness of heaven. Amid the changes and sorrows of life, how delightful it is to anticipate that inheritance which is incorruptible and fadeth not away! Though Providence for a time may mingle nothing but undisguised blessings in his cup; like the patriarch in the land that flowed with milk and honey, the true believer looks forward with a pilgrim's longing for a better, even an heavenly, country. And to the perceptions of faith, verifying the sure word of prophecy, how rich is the substance of things hoped for, how resplendent the evidence of things not seen! What radiancy of glory shines through every word in which the spirit of God has revealed to us the things he has prepared for them that love him! Every beautiful and precious object on earth is a type and a shadow of heaven.

The whole visible universe, with its manifold works of divine wisdom and power, is but a volume of illustrations, leading us by easy steps to the knowledge of that world of infinite love above and beyond the stars. The spirit of all truth has interpreted these pictures with exquisite clearness and grace. The book of Revelation, especially in its closing chapters, is illuminated with a wealth of imagery, beside which all the poet's dreams of the golden age, and all man's uninspired aspirations of the good time coming, are poor and mean. Here is the perfection of all beauty; a light ineffable, to which the sun can add no brightness; a celestial paradise, infinitely surpassing the garden which the Creator's own hand planted eastward in Eden; an eternal city, of which God himself is the builder, the temple, and the light. And the inhabitants of the heavenly world are in harmony with their dwelling-place. For " the nations of them that are saved walk in the light of it." From the feet that tread those golden streets, or wander in the sweet fields of everlasting spring, all defilement is removed and all weariness has departed ; from the eyes that behold those heaven-built walls and fountains of living water God has wiped all tears away; and the voices that flow together in the anthems of celestial rapture know no note of sadness for evermore. O blessed contemplation of unfading glory! O sweet, seraphic vision of perfect purity and peace, of eternal rest, of joy unspeakable! If prayer to our Father in heaven did no more than bring us daily by anticipation to the innumerable company of angels and spirits of the just made perfect, — if it were nothing but the lifting up of the soul by faith from these shadows to that substance, from these husks to that bread in our Father's house, from these perishable ties to that fellowship of unchanging love, — prayer would still be our vital breath. When we express the spirit of adoption before our Father in heaven, and hallow his name, and desire the coming of his kingdom, and crown our supplications with the sincere wish that his will may be done here as it is done in the home of all his ransomed family, we have already mounted up on wings as an eagle into heaven. For what is the essence of heaven's happiness? Why are its inhabitants blessed, even as God is, for evermore? Surely, not because the streets are gold, and the gates pearl, and the foundations all manner of precious stones: these material glories are only the outward exponents of a blessedness which is inward and spiritual. The angels who sang at midnight among the hills of Judah, the messengers who sat all radiant with glory in the vacant tomb of Christ, and all the ministering spirits who go forth to succor the heirs of salvation, whether they throng around the tempted Saviour in the wilderness and the garden, or hover over us in our trials, are as truly happy as when they worship with veiled faces before the throne of God and the Lamb. In heaven above or in earth beneath, the blessedness of perfect spirits depends simply upon the conformity of their will to God's will. They love what he loves, they hate what he hates, they rejoice to do what he commands; and whether they are required to canopy the stony couch of Jacob at Bethel, or to convoy the soul of Lazarus from the rich man's gate to Abraham's bosom, or to sing before the eternal throne, or to lift up the everlasting gates that the King of Glory may come in, the performance of the divine will makes both the song and the service a perpetual delight. In heaven God's will is done spontaneously and perfectly: therefore it *is* heaven. Would we share the happiness of angels? Would we find glory begun below, and be made meet at last for the fellowship of the saints in light? Let us learn to pray intelligently and sincerely, " Thy will be done."

God's will and the creature's will are the two opposing forces of the universe. It is not doubtful which will ultimately triumph. But, meantime, while the conflict lasts, it is the cause of all discord and misery. If we would find the place where spirits blend in the harmony of the blessed, we must come to the mercy-seat with this prayer as the expression of our personal wishes, regarding its fulfilment as the goal of our utmost attainments. For just here, as it seems to us, is the distinction between this petition and the preceding one. When we say, " Thy kingdom come," we take a comprehensive view, and desire the extension of the gospel, the upbuilding of the universal church, the development of grace into glory in ourselves and among all men, so that our Father's name may be universally hallowed. But when we add, " Thy will be done," we make a special application of these comprehensive petitions to ourselves; not, indeed, excluding others, yet praying that we in particular may be enabled to advance, and fitted to enjoy, the consummation and triumph of God's kingdom on earth. And, as in the former petition we have respect not to that divine sovereignty which is in itself perfect and incapable of increase or diminution, but simply to the recognition of that sovereignty in the hearts of men, so now, it is not his *decretive*, but his *declarative* will, to which we desire to be brought into absolute and perfect subjection. This declarative, or revealed will of God concerning us may be regarded in two aspects: first as to its *requirements*, and secondly as to its *inflictions;* for unto us it is given not only to do, but also to suffer, according to the will of God. This distinction is formal rather than substantial. For obedience, whether active or passive, springs from the same root, and grows into the same result. The spirit which inspires an angel's fervent service would constrain him to an entire resignation if he were called upon to suffer. The best examples we have on earth blend active duty with patient endurance. Moses, condemned to die on the borders of Canaan, waits and works till his great change comes ; and then goes up, with unabated strength and an undimmed eye, to his mountain tomb. Jesus Christ, having finished the work the Father had given him to do, pressed the bitter cup to his lips, and said, "Not my will, but thine be done." He whose active obedience is most pure and perfect will be best qualified to endure in the day of trial; and so also, he who has learned obedience by the things he has suffered will be most prompt and perfect in his active duty.

But though the two forms of obedience are thus intimately connected at their base, growing like twin saplings from the same root, it will be most convenient for us to consider them separately.

In reference to active obedience, let it be observed that the great pre-requisite for the doing of God's will from the heart, as it is done in heaven, is a supreme and single regard for his commandment. Angels and glorified saints have no abstract theory of morals. Their philosophy is summed up in the single axiom, "The law of the Lord is perfect." They know nothing of expediency, or the fitness of things, or the light of nature, as constituting the ground of moral obligation. The divine will is to them the perfection of all wisdom, the standard of all duty, the source of all obligations; and when that will is once clearly expressed,

> "Not Gabriel asks the reason why,
> Nor God the reason gives."

It is for this heavenly obedience that our Lord teaches us to pray and to strive. Instead of the vain philosophy which would fain be wise above what is written, and " reasons high of providence, foreknowledge, will and fate, and finds no end in wandering mazes lost," let us practically adopt these simple but sublime principles: God is essentially and infinitely holy, wise, and good; his law is not only the expression of his will, but the transcript of his nature; the written revelation he has given us contains the perfect expression of his will so far as it relates to our conduct and destiny; " the secret things belong unto the Lord our God, but those things which are revealed belong unto us and to our children for ever, that we may do all the words of this law." Therefore whatever the Bible commands us is *right*, *eternally* and *infinitely* right; and whatever the Bible forbids us is *wrong*, *eternally* and *infinitely* wrong: right, not because it accords with reason or tends to promote human welfare (which in the long-run will doubtless appear to be true), but right because God's will, expressing his own perfect nature, ordained it as the rule of our action; wrong, not because man's conscience disapproves it, or man's experience has found it to be evil (this also is doubtless true and important in its place), but wrong because God's law forbids it, and hedges us up from its performance by his threatened punishments.

It is easy to see that this pure respect for the divine authority lies at the foundation of all acceptable duty. It is the sanctifying motive, without which an action, though right in itself, is worthless in God's sight. When a man undertakes to be his own God, and makes his own reason, or taste, or interest the rule of his conduct, — even though his performances should coincide outwardly with the divine requirements, — he is but a worshipper of self, and the smoke of his sacrifice rises no higher than the breath of his own nostrils. To be a saint indeed, is to live our prayer, and make our actions designedly the counterpart of God's will. Just in proportion as this principle is received into a man's intellect and heart, it will pervade his whole being and control all the issues of his life. It will cause him to have respect to *all* the divine commandments. He will not undertake to weigh transgression in the balance of his disordered understanding. He will plead no exemption in favor of what men call little sins. The first table of the law will be as sacred in his sight as the second. He will fear to take God's name in vain, to violate the Sabbath, to neglect any Christian duty, for the same reason that he fears to steal or to murder. He understands that one forbidden fruit, however pleasant it may be to the eyes, may be by divine appointment the test of all obedience; that "if a man keep the whole law, and yet offend in one point, he is guilty of all," because it all rests on the same authority, and because the least commandment is a perfect expression of the divine will no less than the greatest.

Moreover, the obedience of such a man will be prompt and unanswering. To human reason the precept may sometimes seem dark and even cruel. It may command Abraham to bind the son of his old age and the child of promise to the altar of burnt sacrifice. But, if the intimation of God's sovereign will is clearly authenticated, what has Abraham to do with the reason or the result of the requirement, so far as the obligation to obey is concerned? His understanding or approval is not the measure of his duty. He who gives the command will take care of the covenant promise with which it seems to conflict, and silence in his own way the cavilling of the heathen. The order is the explicit will of God, who is infinitely wise and holy; and the finite creature has nothing to do but to obey. So thought the faithful patriarch, as he toiled up the mount of sacrifice, with the dear boy by his side tugging at his heart-strings; and so he thought still, when his stern grief was suddenly turned into joy at the voice from heaven, " Lay not thine hand upon the lad; for now I know thou fearest God, seeing thou hast not withheld thy son, thine only son, from me." The obedience of such a man, however inferior in degree, is of the same kind with that of the angels. He " delights in the law of God after the inward man." He struggles for more complete conformity to it. In his eye the most attractive feature of heaven is the perfect peace which there prevails between the Creator's and the creature's will. He would be there, because he would be free not only from the outward defilement, but from the inward motions of sin, and exercise the faculties of his new nature without hindrance from the old. And thus he literally anticipates heaven. Obedience is to him the key of knowledge and the spring of joy. He knows of the doctrine, because he does his Father's will, and finds that in the keeping of the commandments there is great reward.

We hardly need to be reminded that such a spirit as we have described is not the offspring of our carnal nature. Flesh and blood cannot beget it. Reason cannot attain to it. It is the workmanship and the gift of God through the regenerating power of the Holy Ghost. Nor can the spirit of obedience sustain itself. It must be nourished daily by the same grace that first begets it. God's commandments are exceeding broad. Our strength is small; and many are the foes, both without and within us, who fight against our doing of his will. What better can we do in the consciousness of weakness, and in the stress of conflict, than to take this prayer to the mercy-seat, and say, — " Father, teach me thy will, and enable me to do it. Write thy law upon my heart, and strengthen me to obey it. Give what thou commandest, and then command what thou wilt." The man who thus prays shall be blessed in his deed. The leaf of his obedience shall not wither, nor its fruit fail; for its roots run down deep into the living waters, and the dew of heaven lies all night upon its branches.

In regard to passive obedience, or submission to God's will, it is important, first of all, to understand wherein it consists. It is not indifference to suffering. A Christian and a Stoic have nothing in common. There is no blind chance in Providence, and there is no hard fatalism in the faith that submits to its allotments. "To be above the stroke of suffering is a condition equal to angels; to be in a state of sorrow without the sense of sorrow is a disposition beneath beasts; but duly to regulate our sorrows and bound our passions under the rod is the wisdom, duty, and excellency of a Christian."* God has one Son without sin, but no son without stripes. Affliction is the badge of adoption. The afflicted may be "overwhelmed, and pour out his complaint before the Lord." (Ps. cii.) In all this

* Flavel.

Job sinned not, neither charged God foolishly. Child of sorrow, God does not chide thy tears. Rather would he be offended at the hardness that will not grieve when he smites. He allows and desires thee to weep, if only thou wilt not rebel; to mourn, if thou refusest not to be comforted; to complain *to* him, if only thou dost not complain *against* him. Come with thy sorrows even to his seat, and pour thy tears into his bosom. Only lean hard upon his arm, and look into his face and say from the heart, "Thy will be done."

As passive obedience does not include insensibility to suffering, so neither does it exclude the employment of all lawful means to escape from evil. The law of self-preservation is divine. To inflict penance on ourselves is to invade God's prerogatives, and take the rod out of his fatherly hand. To run rashly into danger, or even to neglect the means of safety and deliverance, is to despise not only our own life, but the bounty and authority of its Author. True Christian faith does not pervert our natural instincts, so that we can say, "Evil, be thou my good;" neither does it dissolve our obligation, nor discourage our efforts, to do ourselves no harm, to abide in the ship, to work out our own temporal and eternal salvation. But, faith undergirds our efforts with a consciousness of absolute dependence on God, and throws over our failures and disappointments a sense of divine wisdom and love that renders submission easy. The true spirit of resignation is illustrated in living Scripture examples more beautifully than it can be set forth in any abstract definition. Most perfect of all is the pattern of the Saviour's patience in suffering. There are two scenes in his life around which Christian memory delights to linger. One is where he stands weeping with human tenderness at the grave of Lazarus, and the other where he falls down and prays with human resignation in the Garden of Gethsemane. Those tears on the Saviour's face, and those agonized yet submissive supplications on the Saviour's lips, — how blessed is the ministry they perform! They come to us in our hour of trial, and assure us that he is our kinsman. When we mourn over those who have fallen asleep, we are reminded that " Jesus wept." When our soul is exceeding sorrowful under the shadow of coming woes, we go out to the Mount of Olives, and hear his strong cries and supplications in the days of his flesh. We are comforted with the assurance of his sympathy: we are reproved and instructed by his example of entire resignation. There is, doubtless, a depth in that agony which made his soul a sacrifice for sin, to which human experience never can descend on this side of hell, and a mystery which we cannot comprehend in that triumph of the divine over the human will in the person of the God-man; yet, on its surface, the awful scene presents this precious lesson: that we may be exceeding sorrowful and agonize in prayer for deliverance, and at the same time leave the whole case to God's disposal, saying, " Not my will, but thine, be done." Aside from its intrinsic excellence and authority, how weighty are the arguments by which the Saviour's example is enforced! To whose will are we required to submit? Shall not the child yield to its Father, the creature to the Creator, the weak to the Omnipotent, the foolish to the All-wise, the ignorant to the Omniscient, the sinful to the infinitely Holy? What are we, but a handful of dust which his breath has quickened? and shall we fly into the face of the Almighty, because he does what he pleases with his own? What have we that we have not received as an unmerited gift? and, amid unnumbered bounties that remain, shall we rise in rebellion because of the few that are removed? Shall not the sea of God's mercies swallow up a few drops of affliction? Should it be according to your mind? Are you competent to govern even the world in which you move? Is there one sun in the heavens whose chariot you would presume to guide, or one grave in the earth over which you would dare to proclaim the resurrection before the time? Poor worm! cease thy vain contention with thy Maker. Be still, and know that he is GOD. Let the thought that he reigns absolutely, rightfully, wisely, and lovingly, come into and possess your soul. This divine thought will not only compose, but strengthen and console you. The sovereignty of God — controlling all things, from the destruction of a world to the fall of a sparrow — is the most comforting truth in the Bible. Oh, when I sit amid the ashes of hopes that have perished, and purposes that have been cut off in a moment; when I stand weeping at the tomb where my own flesh lies mouldering, or look into my own heart upon the yet green graves of joys and affections that have expired, — let not the miserable comforters, who peep and mutter and speculate, disturb the stillness of that holy twilight with their windy talk. I want none of your learned babbling about chance and fortune, about life-forces and disease, and the course of nature; none of your shallow truisms about something worse that might have happened, or something better that may be in store: but help me, if you can, to hear the still, small voice of God; to look up, and believe like a child that my Father in heaven, sovereign and irresistible, yet wise and pitiful, quenched that precious life, and dug that dark grave, and disposes of every particle of that sleeping dust. Let me see the broad seal of my King on the stone of the sepulchre; let me forget the Chaldeans and Sabeans, the wind from the wilderness and the fire out of heaven, and realize only that the "*Lord* hath taken away;" and this great thought will quiet my soul like the voice of Christ upon the waters. I shall be perfectly still, when I can say, *Thou didst it.* And in that stillness of the heart under the shadow of the Almighty, how the revelations of his purposes will come out one by one, and shine in their well-ordered frame, like the stars in the quiet heavens after the sun has gone down! All things work together for good to them that love God, to them who are the called according to his purpose. For this is his will concerning us, even our sanctification. As we hallow his name, so would he hallow our nature. In his sovereignty he is still our Father. He doth not afflict wantonly, but for our good, that we may be partakers of his holiness. The Captain of our salvation was made perfect through sufferings; and the sons whom he would bring to glory must indeed be baptized with his baptism and drink of his cup. Sharp as the ingredients of that cup may be, the assurance that it is mingled by a Father's hand for our good neutralizes its bitterness and turns its sorrow into joy. In the darkest providences, the promise shines like the rainbow on the clouds. God lines the yoke with comfort, and gives honey at the end of the rod. "Thy will be done" is not the mere utterance of blind submission. It is the voice of that peace with God which glories in tribulation also. The martyrs of Jesus praise him in the fires; and while he brings many sons to glory, he glorifies himself before the world by their endurance of suffering. The testimony of the centurion at the cross, "**Surely** this *was* the Son of God," has been wrung time and again from the lips of many witnesses by the patience of his disciples. It was thus the blood of the martyrs became the seed of the church; and thus God writes in many a prisoner's cell, and in many a chamber of sickness and want, those living epistles which are more eloquent and powerful than all the productions of philosophy.

When Milton was smitten with blindness in the meridian of his life and usefulness, the first gathering of that deep darkness cast its shadow upon his soul: complaints rose to his lips, and he exclaimed, "Doth God exact day-labor, light denied?"

> " But Patience, to prevent
> That murmur, soon replied: 'God doth not need
> Either man's works, or his own gifts; who best
> Bear his mild yoke, they serve him best; his state
> Is kingly; thousands at his bidding speed,
> And post o'er land and ocean without rest:
> They also serve who only stand and wait.'"

Write that golden line upon our chamber-walls and over the door-posts of our hearts: —

> "They also serve who only stand and wait."

Let us have, even in days of prosperity, some

quiet spot and some hours rescued from the turmoil of life, which shall be to us like the shadow of the olive-trees in the Garden of Gethsemane. There let us learn to say, " Thy will be done." Alas for the man who, when trouble comes, does not know where or how to go and pour out his tears upon his Father's bosom! It cools the feverish brow, and quiets the agitated soul, to weep at the mercy-seat like a child at home. It smooths the grim features of approaching danger, when we can go familiarly to God, and say, " Be not far from me, for trouble is near." And especially it gives present peace, ripening into everlasting joy, when amid the swelling waves and raging storm we can lie down in the everlasting arms, with no thought, no desire, no hope, but this: " Thy will be done on earth as it is in heaven."

"When languor and disease invade
This trembling house of clay,
'Tis sweet to look beyond our pains,
And long to flee away;

"Sweet on his faithfulness to rest,
Whose love can never end;
Sweet on his covenant of grace
For all things to depend;

" Sweet in the confidence of faith
 To trust his firm decrees ;
 Sweet to lie passive in his hands,
 And know no will but his.

" If such the sweetness of the streams,
 What must the fountain be,
 Where saints and angels draw their bliss
 Immediately from thee ! "

CHAPTER V.

" Give us this Day our Daily Bread."

THE Lord's prayer divides itself at this point into two parts: the first relating primarily to God's glory, that he in all things may have the pre-eminence; and the second giving greater prominence to the expression of our personal necessities. Yet the two parts are not so separated as to be disconnected in their fundamental meaning, but only divided as the waves are divided from the sea. The several petitions everywhere overlap and flow into each other.

In the second, as in the first group, there is a progression and a climax. In the first we descend from the hallowing of God's name, through the coming of his kingdom, to the complete fulfilment of his will in us. Here we are brought to the consciousness of our weakness and insufficiency. The sublime rapture of the soul in the contemplation of the divine glory is interrupted by the sense of those personal wants, which not only render us needy in ourselves, but unfit us for our destiny as the children and the heirs of God. The voice of our prayer, therefore, descends from the high notes of adoration and praise to the lowest and deepest tones of supplication.

The petition before us is the profoundest depth to which infinite wisdom has come down to interpret and to encourage us in the utterance of our wants. We are here taught to cry to our Father in heaven from the very lowest parts of the earth, even from the infirmities of our perishing bodies and the beggarly elements which sustain them. But, having reached this lowest point, we are not to tarry here. There is in this ladder of prayer an ascending, as well as a descending climax. From the bread that perishes, faith goes up again to that which endures; to the blessedness of forgiven sin, to the exercise of divine forgiveness, and finally to that entire deliverance from all evil which will qualify the praying soul perfectly to do God's will, and to hallow his name with all saints and holy angels in his kingdom.

Simple as this petition, " Give us this day our daily bread," appears, there is perhaps no verse in the Bible which has been the theme of more earnest discussion, or has given rise to a greater variety of interpretations. And the reason for these differences is to be found, as it seems to us, not in any accidental obscurity in the words, but in the intended depth of their meaning; even as the great and wide sea, in its crystalline clearness, looks darker than some turbid but shallow stream. One chief point of discussion in the interpretation is the precise meaning of the original word translated "daily." This word (ἐπιούσιος) is not found in any of the classic Greek writers, and occurs nowhere in the New Testament, except in the Lord's prayer. Deriving no light whatever from usage, interpreters are shut up to the simple consideration of its etymology. And here there is great diversity of opinion. But the most approved and judicious among modern writers on the subject seem to be agreed that it is most probably the adjective form of a noun which signifies *existence* or *subsistence*. The phrase *daily bread* is therefore equivalent to the *bread of subsistence;* i.e., the bread which is necessary and proper for the support of our life. In some versions of the Scripture the petition is more accurately rendered, "Give us our *needful* bread this day."

Another ground of controversy is the meaning of the word "bread." Here, also, opinions are various, embracing two opposite extremes. Some have insisted that the word is to be taken in its most literal sense, as referring only to the food that nourishes our bodies. Others have gone so far in the opposite direction as to exclude the literal sense entirely, and insist that it refers only to our spiritual nourishment, "to that bread which cometh down from heaven, of which if a man eat he shall never die." Among the early Christian writers, commonly called "the fathers," who were all more or less given to a mystical interpretation of Scripture, there was a prevalent opinion that this petition contains a mysterious and profound reference to the Lord's Supper. Hence, in course of time, the use of the whole prayer was restricted to communicants; and its repetition by others was regarded as profane. And perhaps this opinion was one chief reason for the long prevalent practice of administering the Lord's Supper every day, so that the bread of the communion might be literally the believer's *daily* bread. Now, without going into the formal discussion of the subject, we think that the true answer to both these extreme views, and the demonstration of our Lord's true meaning in teaching us to ask daily for our needful bread, may be found in the nature and design of the whole prayer. It is not, as we have before shown, a rigid and invariable *form*, but a *model*, giving choice specimens, and embodying the true spirit of all prayer. It matters not, therefore, whether we take the word " bread " in its most literal and restricted, or in its most spiritual and comprehensive sense: the ultimate meaning is the same. If we take it, figuratively, to signify nourishment in general, it certainly includes bodily as well as spiritual food. The objection, that Christ would not teach us to ask for so small a thing as the bread that perishes, is not only frivolous, but inconsistent with spiritual piety. How much better are we than the fowls of the air! Our heavenly Father, who feedeth them, careth also for the least want of his children. Whatever is not beneath him to bestow is not improper for us to ask. Indeed, the best proof of our faith is the recognition of his fatherly kindness, as extending to the smallest matters, and taking care even of our perishing bodies.

If, on the other hand, we take the word "bread" literally (and we think this, because it is the simplest and most natural, is also the best way), it is then but a *specimen* of our wants, suggestive of all our need as dependent creatures; and the fact that Christ teaches us to ask literally for bread is both our instruction and our encouragement to go to our heavenly Father for the supply of all our necessities, bodily and spiritual, temporal and eternal. The intelligent and devout consideration of our own dependence, and of God's infinite bounty in the supply of our lowest wants, is the first and most necessary step towards the apprehension of all our necessities, and of all his infinite mercies. There is, therefore, a profound wisdom in putting the simple word "bread" in the first petition of the second table of prayer. As soon as we begin to eat we should begin to pray. As long as we eat we should continue our supplications, with an ever deepening and widening sense of our dependence, until at last our hunger for the bread that perishes is swallowed up and lost in the desire and enjoyment of that which endures to everlasting life.

The petition before us is like a simple

flower, in whose beautiful unity many leaves are skilfully enfolded. Every word is a doctrine, a precept, and a promise. And even as the holy incense of the ancient sanctuary was compounded of many precious spices and perfumes, many Christian graces are mingled, and ascend before God from the altar of the heart, whenever this prayer is sincerely and intelligently offered.

I. We come to our heavenly Father, and say, GIVE. Here is the recognition of our true relation to God, — the acknowledgment of our obligations to him, the profession of our gratitude for all his benefits. In the very act of asking, we confess that we have nothing which we have not received, and that we can receive nothing worth having which he does not bestow. Every good and perfect gift is from above, and cometh down from the Father of lights. And though our gross hearts are slow to believe it, this is just as true of temporal as of spiritual blessings. He feeds and clothes us, even as the fowls of the air and the lilies of the field; opens for us the gates of every morning, and curtains our repose every evening; quickens our pulses with the glow of health, and makes all our bed in our sickness;

heals all our diseases, and crowns us with loving-kindness and tender mercies; satisfies our mouth with good things, and renews our youth like the eagle's. In him we live and move and have our being. The Scriptures assert and illustrate this great truth in a thousand ways. Right reason approves and confirms the Bible doctrine; and the same arguments by which men in their self-sufficiency would exclude the agency and bounty of God from the details of their every-day life, if logically carried out, would lead to absolute atheism. But we will not argue the point. Our business now is to meditate devoutly on the admitted truth. How glorious and blessed is the vision, when we think of God seated on the throne of the universe, clothed with majesty and girded with strength, yet omnipresent and all-pervading and infinitely loving, fixing his paternal eye upon the humblest of his creatures, and opening his all-bountiful hand to supply the wants of every living thing! Overshadowed and filled with this precious thought, look out upon some populous landscape, when it is clothed in the soft beauty of the mellowing year. The wheat-field, tinged with yellow, swells in the breeze like a golden sea; the

THE MODEL PRAYER. 107

tasselled corn waves its banners of peace and plenty; and the orchard begins to bend under the growing burden of its fruit. As your heart broods and dilates upon the beauty of the scene, the cloud, which was no bigger than your hand, has expanded, and overspread the heavens, and dispenses its treasures in drops more precious than pearls. Again, the sun breaks out, and sets God's bow in the cloud, the seal of his covenant concerning seed-time and harvest. Who can look upon such a picture; who can follow the influence of that sunshine and shower, through all the varying beauty of the landscape, to the homes of men, and think how every drop of rain puts food into the mouth of a hungry child, how every ray of light sends its merriment to the table of health, and its quickening power into the chamber of sickness,— without profound gratitude to God who crowns the year with his goodness, " and spreads a common feast for all that live"?

How base and unnatural is the ungodliness of men! An earthly father, in any wise worthy of the name, is never entirely forgotten. The most wayward and prodigal son will sometimes turn back with a tender remembrance to the home of his childhood, and melt at the recollection of paternal goodness. But alas! our Father in heaven who, never weary of giving, makes his sun to rise on the evil and on the good, and sends rain on the just and on the unjust,—how is he despised and forgotten! Men pollute with their boasting and profanity the very air with which he fans their lungs and vitalizes their blood. They live and move amid the tokens of his loving care, and yet exclude him from their thoughts.

> " Swinish Gluttony
> Ne'er looks to Heaven amidst his gorgeous feast,
> But, with besotted, base ingratitude,
> Crams, and blasphemes his Feeder."

This ingratitude of the creature towards the Creator is monstrous and horrible. The dumb things of creation might well be moved when the almighty Father lifts up his voice, and complains, saying, "Hear, O heavens, and be astonished, O earth: I have nourished and brought up children, and they have rebelled against me." From this reproach even the adopted and praying children of God are not entirely exempt. How often do we form our worldly plans without reference to our dependence on his blessing! How often do we attribute our temporal successes to our own skill rather than to his bounty! How often, when we have contributed of our abundance to his cause, do we feel that we have conferred a favor on him, and come even to his mercy-seat in the spirit of a claimant, and not of a suppliant! When such feelings have dominion over us, the use of the Lord's prayer is a mockery and an insult. Let us strive to realize our true position as the recipients of his gifts. If we bring all we have to consecrate it on his altar, let us say with David, when he surveyed the treasures he and his people had contributed to the temple: "All things come from thee, and of thine own have we given thee." When we pray for future blessings, let us not forget the undeserved bounties that have crowned the past. Every moment of life has borne to us a rich burden of gifts. All our days we have been pensioners upon his care, breathing his air, rejoicing in his sunshine, feeding upon the fruits of his earth. The debt we owe exceeds not only our ability to pay, but our power to calculate. And still our cry is, *Give, give.* Surely the least we can do is to crown our petitions with a vow: "If God will indeed be with me, and will keep me in the way that I go, and will give me bread to eat, and raiment to put on, then shall the Lord be my God; and of all that thou shalt give me, I will surely give the tenth unto thee."

II. The spirit of true charity, which pervades every part of the Lord's prayer, comes out with special prominence in this petition. Though we may repeat it in solitude, we come to God as *our* Father, and say, " Give us our daily bread." The selfish man, who has no wish to gratify beyond the circle of his own wants, can never offer this prayer sincerely. He has not comprehended the first elements of the gospel, nor experienced the first workings of genuine grace. The religion of Christ is tender, and pitiful, and large-hearted. It intensifies, and at the same time extends, a man's natural affections; makes him love and provide for his own more earnestly, and yet enlarges the circumference of his sympathies to embrace the household of faith, and pity the world that lieth in wickedness. The great Teacher interprets the language of the Christian heart when he instructs us to say, " Our Father, give us our daily bread." Gross is the incongruity of such a prayer upon lips that are daily familiar with evil speaking and bitterness. Gross is the hypocrisy of the man who thus speaks to God, while he fills his heart with malice and exclusive pride towards his fellow-men, turns a deaf ear to the claims of the destitute, and drives on his selfish schemes with cold indifference to the prosperity and happiness of others. It behooves us to keep our hearts with all diligence against the hardening influences of the world. The rivalries of trade, the vanities of fashion, the pride of birth and social position, are powerful stimulants to the selfishness of our nature. The old man, with his deceitful lusts, needs to be mortified by giving to others, even as we ask God to give to us. " Charge them that are rich in this world, that they be not high-minded, nor trust in uncertain riches, but in the living God, who giveth us richly all things to enjoy; that they do good, that they be rich in good works, ready to distribute, willing to communicate." If we would not be hardened and destroyed by God's gifts to us, let us seek, beyond ourselves and the narrow circle of our own, for objects on which to bestow the tokens of our gratitude. Visit the fatherless and the widow in their affliction, become God's almoners through whom he may answer the supplications of the poor, and so prove the sincerity of your prayer when you say, "Give us this day our daily bread."

III. The petition before us is the embodiment of that Christian moderation by which the precepts and promises of the Bible are everywhere pervaded. We are taught to ask, not for dainties, but for *bread;* not for superfluous, but for daily, or *necessary*, bread; which being interpreted means, " a competent portion of the good things of this life, and God's blessing with them."

It is right to pray for whatever it is lawful to pursue. We may ask God for worldly prosperity, for health and riches, and whatever contributes to our temporal well-being. But, then, let it ever be remembered that our petitions for these earthly things should differ in several respects from the supplications we offer for spiritual blessings.

When we ask for pardon and peace and sanctifying grace, — knowing that the bestowal of these things is in accordance with God's will, and that their possession to the utmost degree can do us nothing but good, — we may pray absolutely, and with an importunity which will take no denial. But as we know nothing of God's will concerning our future prosperity in this world, and are incapable of judging how far temporal success would be consistent with the highest good of our souls, our prayers for the good things of this life should always be conditional, uttered in a spirit of resignation, and qualified with the express proviso, "nevertheless not my will, but thine, be done."

Moreover, temporal blessings are to be sought not only conditionally, but with a view to their consecration to spiritual uses; while the gifts of divine grace to the soul are, in themselves, satisfying and lasting as the mind, and therefore infinitely to be desired for their own sake. The bread that perishes in the using, and the riches that moth and rust corrupt, are desirable only as means to the attainment of higher ends. Even a heathen philosopher could say, "I do not live to eat, but eat to live;" and the apothegm may well be applied by a Christian to all temporal blessings, as the support and nourishment of his spiritual and eternal life. If we ask for any thing that we may consume it upon our lusts, however refined or intrinsically innocent the form of the consumption may be, we ask amiss;

and it will prove in the end a mercy to us not to receive.

And, furthermore, when we ask for temporal good in submission to God's will, and with a view to use it for spiritual ends, we must still be moderate in our desires. To estimate the good things of this life at their real worth, and to use the world as not abusing it, has always been a rare and difficult attainment. The difficulty is greatly enhanced by the spirit of the times in which we live. It is no easy thing to avoid the contagious influence of the social extravagance which is sweeping over the world with the violence of an epidemic disease. Everywhere men seem bent on demonstrating the proposition that a man's life *does* consist in the abundance of the things which he possesses. The popular notion as to what constitutes a worldly competency has undergone a great and ruinous change during the past few years. The style in which our fathers lived, and from which many of them transmitted to us a character more precious than gold, has become contemptible in the eyes of their children. Success in life is made synonymous with the rapid accumulation and the vulgar display of material wealth. The worth of a man and his social standing are estimated not so much by the excellency of what he is, as by the abundance of what he has; while his knowledge, his refinement, and even his virtue, are put in the lowest place of the scale by which he is measured. This prevalent materialism is most pernicious in its influence upon all the interests of time and eternity. It is the bane of all true social enjoyment. The pride and envy it begets sit like veiled skeletons at every feast. Covetousness is the most exacting and onerous of all idolatries. He is not poor that hath little; but he that desireth much. It is the bitter fountain of untold crimes and miseries; for "they that will be rich fall into temptation and a snare, and into many foolish and hurtful lusts." Above all, it is the enemy and the destruction of all gratitude to God, contentment with his providence, and liberality to his cause. They whose hearts are set on riches, whether in the pursuit or the possession, can never repeat the Lord's prayer in spirit and in truth, nor discharge the obligations of God's children to their Father in heaven and their brethren on earth. Our security against innumerable dangers, temporal and spiritual, is found in the moderation of our desires. For even in this world a man " does not live by bread alone." It is doubtless well, when the use of great possessions can be added to a cultivated mind, and a liberal heart and fervent spirit in God's service ; but how rare are such combinations ! How hardly do they who have riches enter into the kingdom of heaven, in this world or the next! What are called the middle walks of life are generally the safest; and to the great majority of Christians the petition before us finds its true interpretation in the prayer of Agur : " Remove far from me vanity and lies ; give me neither poverty nor riches ; feed me with food convenient for me : lest I be full, and deny thee, and say, Who is the Lord? or lest I be poor, and steal, and take the name of my God in vain."

IV. It was evidently the Saviour's design that the prayer he has given us should be a model of our daily supplications, and that it should embody a sense of continual dependence on God for all things pertaining to life and godliness. "This day" qualifies and limits all the petitions. We are to approach the throne of grace for the supply of our present wants, pledging ourselves to be content with what is sufficient for us now, and purposing to renew the application with the return of our necessities. God nowhere promises to give either temporal or spiritual blessings in advance, but reserves to himself the fatherly prerogative to spread our table, and proportion our grace, according to our day. He would thus cultivate in us a sense of absolute and continual dependence.

This, of course, does not forbid the exercise of a prudent forethought; neither does it excuse indolence, or neglect of daily business. For it is a law, no less binding than the obligation to pray, that, "if any man will not work, neither should he eat." In the petition we are considering, we ask for *our* bread, — the bread which is appropriate to us by the divine blessing on our own exertions; not the bread of idleness, nor of violence, nor of deceit; not the bread which belongs to our neighbor, and which we have extorted from him by a shrewd trick of trade, or a cunning appeal to his sympathies; not the bread which some great scheme of legalized robbery has snatched from the mouths of the widow and the fatherless: but *our* bread, coming down to us like manna from heaven, yet gathered by our own diligence in a business in whose minutest details we are not ashamed to ask God to prosper us. But, while it is consistent with and requires diligence in business and a prudent foresight, this divine prayer condemns all such anxious care for the future as leads to a distrust of divine providence. A gloomy disposition which looks on the dark side of every picture, and poisons the enjoyment of present abundance with the anticipation of future want, is utterly at variance with the childlike trust the Saviour would inculcate. Alas, how reluctant we are to take God at his word, to cast our burden upon him, to do our duty, and leave the result to his disposal! How slow we are to learn the lesson which blooms for us in every flower of the field, is chanted in every wild bird's song, illustrated in every phase of Christian experience, and written in letters of light upon every page of the Bible! A thousand times have we been taught the folly of being " over-exquisite to cast the fashion of uncertain evil;" a thousand times have we heard the gray-headed saint testify, "I have been young, and now am I old; yet have I not seen the righteous forsaken, nor his seed begging bread:" and yet our stupid hearts refuse to repose on the promises.

THE MODEL PRAYER.

We are not willing that God should keep the storehouse of plenty under his lock and key, and dispense its fulness according to his own judgment of our wants. We would fain have his gifts in advance, measured out to us not according to our needs, but according to our fears. And thus we continually bring the imaginary shadows of to-morrow over the real sunshine of to-day, and poison the sweet cup of present plenty with the anticipation of future want.

And if such distrust be inconsistent with the true spirit of prayer, much more is the pride which affects to be independent of Providence. This is the great sin of prosperity. "Now," says the successful man, "I ask no favors. I have much goods laid up for many days. I have put a nail in the wheel of fortune." God, who hears the thoughts of the heart, often listens to such atheism as this; and, in mercy to his people, he smites the gourd under whose shadow it is cherished. Fortunes, rolled up like a snowball, melt away like snow in the sun. And however the fact may be explained, in one view of it, by the weakness of men who grow giddy with success, we are sure the finger of our Father is in it;

and the vicissitudes of fortune are the execution of his merciful designs to his chosen. The fool may be suffered to go on in his merry atheism till his soul is required of him; but God's children must be brought in time to feel their dependence. "Give us this day our daily bread" is not only the poor man's prayer: it is no less appropriate to the rich. The largest portion of the good things of this life ceases to be a competency, unless God's blessing comes with it. Though our estate be as secure as human wisdom can make it, we need daily to acknowledge and seek benedictions from the great Benefactor, lest in mercy to our souls he recall the gifts for which we forget to be grateful, or in wrath continue them only as a judgment on our folly. The communion-table is not the only place where men eat and drink damnation to themselves. Any table may become a snare. Fulness of bread and forgetfulness of God may make any house like Sodom and Gomorrah; and pride, which is the intoxication of the soul, is no less fatal than bodily drunkenness.

This, then, is the conclusion of the whole matter: that God would have us look up, with a childlike gratitude, to the hand that feeds us, and lean with filial confidence on the arm of Him who pitieth us, even as a father pitieth his children. This is at once our security and our blessedness, when we can sing, "The Lord is my shepherd; I shall not want." For this sense of dependence on God, and of trust in his promises, — cultivated in the first instance at the lowest point of our temporal necessities, where, in fact, it is often most difficult, — pervades and controls the whole course of a Christian's experience. The faith that trusts for daily bread, and the divine gratitude that puts joy and gladness into the heart more than when corn and wine abound to the ungodly, rise into higher spheres, and take hold upon broader and more precious promises. The same hand that gives daily bread gives also daily grace, according to the same wise economy; and the same habit that trusts for temporal, trusts also for spiritual blessings, — for living grace while life lasts, for dying grace in a dying day, and for eternal life when grace is swallowed up in glory. To the confiding and thankful soul the least gift is the pledge and the earnest of the greatest. Nay: the least is ours, because the greatest *has been* bestowed. " He that spared not his own Son, but delivered him up for us all, how shall he not with him also freely give us all things?" All things *are* yours. The Bread which came down from heaven for the life of the world is to those who receive him the pledge that all other things will be added unto them. "My God shall supply all your need according to his riches in glory by Jesus Christ." Let us learn, therefore, to trust and not be afraid.

> "Why should the soul a drop bemoan,
> Who has a fountain near, —
> A fountain which shall ever flow
> With waters sweet and clear?
>
> "No good in creatures can be found,
> But may be found in thee:
> I must have all things and abound,
> While God is God to me.
>
> "He who has made my heaven secure
> Will here all good provide:
> While Christ is rich, can I be poor?
> What can I want beside?
>
> "O Lord, I cast my care on thee!
> I triumph and adore:
> Henceforth my great concern shall be
> To love and praise thee more."

CHAPTER VI.

"*And forgive our Debts, as we forgive our Debtors.*"

"*And forgive us our Sins; for we also forgive every one that is indebted to us.*"

WE have seen that the bread for which we pray in the preceding petition includes, or at least represents, much more than the nourishment of the body, which is soon cut down, and withereth as a flower of the field. We are not to labor, neither are we to pray, chiefly for the meat that perishes, but for that which endureth unto everlasting life. When a disciple of Christ comes to spread out his wants before our Father in heaven, the cravings of natural appetite are intimately connected with hunger and thirst after righteousness. They blend together in one prayer, even as the body and soul are united in one person, and the wants of both in one consciousness. Moreover, temporal and spiritual blessings proceed from the same Source. He who gives daily bread gives also daily grace, ripening continually into eternal glory. He bestows the lesser gift upon his own children, as the pledge and earnest of the greater. And hence the particle, which marks the transition from the preceding petition to the one we are now considering, is not disjunctive, but copulative. The prayer does not say, "Give us our daily bread, *but* grant us also forgiveness and deliverance from evil," as though there were a conflict between our temporal and eternal welfare: it asks for daily bread *and* forgiveness; recognizing the profound fact that, in the economy of divine grace, the body is for *the soul*, temporal bounties in order to spiritual; and that without God's gracious blessing, of which forgiveness is the first-fruits, even a competent portion of this world's good things will, in the end, prove to be only a curse. Unless it be seasoned with a sense of pardoning mercy, they that believe cannot " eat their meat with gladness and singleness of heart;" for they know that a pampered body, with a lean soul, is no better than an ox prepared for the slaughter, or a condemned prisoner fed with dainties while the day of his execution draws

THE MODEL PRAYER. 125

nigh. In this petition for pardon, the spirit of humility and self-abnegation which pervades the whole prayer comes out in bold relief. Here we take the attitude not only of a suppliant, but of a sinner. In the former petition, we confess our need: here we acknowledge our ill desert. Then we cried, *Give:* now our supplication takes a deeper tone, and we cry, *Forgive.* The poverty of spirit, which is the condition of the first beatitude, has ripened into the godly mourning, which is the attribute of the second. The Lord's prayer is, therefore, but a mockery in the lips of a Pharisee, who denies his sinfulness, or of a formalist, who bows the knee before God without a sense of sin in his soul. Here, as in the sacrifices of the old economy, there is a daily remembrance of sins. (Heb. x. 3.) And this remembrance is appropriate to a Christian during the whole period of his earthly discipline. Neither the Antinomian, who denies his obligation to the law of God, as a rule of life, nor the Perfectionist, who claims to be entirely free from sin, can ever use this prayer sincerely. No wonder if they reject it as inconsistent with what they call the freedom of the gospel. "If Christ enjoins on us, during the whole course of our lives, to implore pardon, who can tolerate those new teachers, who, by the phantom of perfect innocence, endeavor to dazzle the simple, and make them believe that they can render themselves completely free from guilt? This, as John declares, is nothing else than to make God a liar."* Furthermore, this prayer has written, on the very face of it, the condemnation of those who, by works of pretended merit, by their own penances and other superstitious observances, undertake to offset and render satisfaction for their sins. They put themselves out of the circle of God's free-forgiveness, and assume to stand upon their own merits before his commutative justice. Nor is this condemnation less obvious in its application to those who go for absolution to any beside our Father in heaven, who only can forgive sins.

But we need not pursue this negative application of the petition before us to the false doctrines and commandments of men. If we can imbue our minds with its positive spirit, all such errors will vanish, as darkness fades before the morning light. Two points claim our attention: first, the *nature of forgiveness*,

* Calvin.

here presented under the figure of cancelling debts; and, secondly, the *force of the argument* involved in the phrase "as we forgive our debtors."

One chief excellency of holy Scripture is its frequent repetition of substantial truth with circumstantial variety; which precludes the suspicion of collusion between the sacred writers, and at the same time makes the Bible itself the best of all commentaries. By "comparing spiritual things with spiritual," the meaning of many a passage, which would otherwise be obscure, becomes luminous and plain. This is strikingly true in regard to the two points now under consideration.

The term "debts" as expressive of our obligations to God, and the corresponding phrase "our debtors" as applied to human relationships, if they stood alone, might well be involved in obscurity and disputes. For *debts*, in its broadest and most common acceptation, is synonymous with *duties*, or *whatever we owe;* and if there were no inspired restriction imposed upon it, licentious interpreters might plausibly insist that we are here taught to pray for deliverance from all duty, and a complete emancipation from the obligations of the divine law. But, as if to anticipate such a perversion, immediately after the first utterance of the Lord's prayer, the Saviour proceeds to expound and restrict this petition in the following words: "For if ye forgive men their *trespasses*, your heavenly Father will forgive you; but if ye forgive not men their *trespasses*, neither will your heavenly Father forgive your *trespasses*." "Trespasses" are more literally *lapses* or *failures in duty*, whether wilful or unintentional. The word occurs frequently in the New Testament, and is translated by *fall, fault*, and *offence*.

The Saviour further interprets his meaning in the second delivery of the Lord's prayer (Luke xi. 4), where the petition is, "And forgive us our *sins*, for we also forgive every one that is *indebted* to us." We are not to suppose, however, that the two words *debts* and *sins* are precisely synonymous. The use of the former phrase is figurative; and the point of the analogy is in the resemblance between the condition of an insolvent debtor, who, unless his debts are cancelled, is liable to be thrown into prison until he has paid the uttermost farthing, and the liability of a sinner to punishment under the divine law he has broken. We owe God a debt of perfect obedience: from *that* obligation we never can be, and no Christian will ever desire to be, absolved. But having failed to pay all the duty we owe, we have incurred a debt of everlasting punishment. We owe God the *penalty* which his law exacts from every transgressor for the vindication of his immutable justice. It is from this penal obligation that we ask to be absolved, when we pray, Forgive us our debts, our trespasses, our sins. And just here we see the true nature of divine forgiveness. It does not relinquish nor relax the claims of the divine law upon us, nor obliterate the fact that we are justly liable to the penalty denounced against any and every transgression: it only releases the sinner from *guilt* in the strict legal sense of the word; *i.e.*, from liability to punishment. After the act of pardon is passed, the claims of the divine law upon the perfect obedience of our heart and life, during the whole continuance of our being, still stand unimpaired; and the fact that we have sinned and come under the condemnation of the law can never be obliterated. Every one of our sins still deserves what every unforgiven sin will surely bring upon the transgressor, — " God's wrath and curse in this life and that which is to come." Though by the act of pardon he gives us, and by his fatherly forgiveness daily renews to us, a receipt in full which exempts us from the payment of that penalty, the evidence of our debt is not blotted out; nay, the very form of the receipt keeps it in continual remembrance. The songs of apostles and martyrs before the throne rehearse with ecstatic gratitude the bondage from which they are redeemed, and the pollution from which they are washed by the blood of Christ. The debts from which we ask to be released, and which in the very asking we continually acknowledge, are infinitely beyond our ability to pay. The penalty of the law is perpetual as its obligation to obedience; and both are infinite and eternal as God, of whose nature that law is the perfect transcript. Though we should suffer the stings of conscience and endure. every conceivable penance during every hour of our earthly life, and then after death lift up our eyes with the rich man in the unalleviated flames of God's penal justice, after untold millions of ages had rolled away, our debts would still be infinite. Our only relief, therefore, is to be found in that divine forgiveness, which, while it does not destroy the fact nor the evidence of our penal debts, does nevertheless cancel and annul our obligation to pay them.

How unspeakable is the benefit conferred upon those who are thus forgiven! It is the most costly, the most comprehensive, the most precious gift, the Creator can bestow on a sinful creature. For be it remembered that our release from the penalty of the violated law is not a mere sovereign act of divine clemency without any satisfaction to offended justice. Neither is the majesty of the law vindicated, nor its claims satisfied, by our prayers or subsequent obedience. Forgiveness is not so cheap a thing as that we can purchase it, nor so lawless as to be given at the sacrifice of truth and justice. Not with silver or gold, or any corruptible thing, not with the tears and sufferings and efforts of man or angel, but with the precious blood of the incarnate Son of God, were we redeemed from the curse of the law. It cost more to secure our forgiveness than it did to build and garnish the whole visible universe. And now, having been bought at such a price, how freely is it bestowed upon us! "In Christ we have remission of sins," "not according to our works, but according to the riches of his grace." The objection that the doctrine of Christ's penal sufferings as our legal substitute destroys the gracious freedom of God's pardoning mercy, and makes the gospel only another phase of the law, is scarcely worthy of serious consideration. The all-sufficient answer is found in the fact that the satisfaction which was rendered to the divine law in our behalf was *not provided by us*, but by the infinitely Holy One against whom we have offended; and that it was provided by him with a view to conserve his own justice, even while he forgives the sinner's debts; and therefore our pardon flows to us freely, in answer to prayer and in fulfilment of gracious promises, from the infinite fountain of that same love which bestowed the gift of a Saviour. And being given thus freely as the purchase of Christ's obedience and death, it must needs be full and everlasting. Since we have "redemption through his blood, even the forgiveness of sins according to the riches of his grace," we may well believe that we are "justified from all things" and can never "fall into condemnation." The forgiven soul may daily sin, and come under God's fatherly displeasure, and so need a daily renewal of the joys of salvation at the mercy-seat; but he can never come again under the divine wrath and curse. His Father in heaven may visit his transgressions with the rod of correction, "nevertheless his loving-kindness will he not utterly take from him, nor suffer his faithfulness to fail." The forgiveness of sins is the pledge of all spiritual blessings. Like a tree of life it stands in the garden of God's delights, thrusting its roots downwards, and lifting its branches upwards laden with precious fruits. It is preceded and followed by the graces of the Spirit, the joys of salvation, the glories of heaven. "O the blessednesses of the man to whom the Lord imputeth not iniquity!" When the Psalmist would stir up his soul to praise God's holy name for his benefits, the first item in the long catalogue is, "who forgiveth all thy iniquities." This is the crowning gift, without which all others are in vain. This sweetens and sanctifies all the bounties of Providence, and makes them blessings indeed. To an unforgiven soul all things are poisoned. His prosperity will destroy him. There is a curse on his houses and lands, on his table and his bed; and when he lifts up his eyes in the eternal world it will only torment him to remember that in this life "he had his good things." When the spirit of God truly convinces a man of sin, this torment is anticipated. What a world of woe is an awakened and guilty conscience! It darkens the fairest prospects with a fearful looking for of judgment. But when that load of sin is gone, and the soul sits by the cross of Christ, conscious of a full and everlasting forgiveness through his blood, who can describe the sweet peace of conscience, the joy in the Holy Ghost, that hushes all its sorrows, and sheds new light over all the relations of life! The bounties of Providence have a new beauty and sweetness now, for they are the tokens of a Father's love. He who forgives all the iniquities will heal all the diseases of the soul, will satisfy our mouth with good things here, and renew our youth like the eagle's in the immortality of heaven. If we would receive this divine forgiveness, let us ask for it. But see to it that ye ask not amiss. Ask not in the spirit of the Pharisee. Learn to estimate your guilt in the light of God's holy law. Honestly believe that you deserve everlasting punishment. And, under a sense of utter ill desert, ask in the name of Christ. "For whatsoever ye shall ask in my name, that will I do, that the Father may be glorified in the Son."

Moreover, if we would have boldness of access and the assurance of acceptance in prayer, we must cultivate in our conduct the evidence of our penitence and of our faith in Christ. And just here, we think, the latter clause of the petition before us comes in; "as we forgive our debtors." What is the precise force and meaning of that *as?* Certainly, it does not indicate the meritorious ground upon which we are to hope for pardon, as though we had a right to claim forgiveness from God in *reward* for our forgiveness of our fellow-men. Neither does it measure the *kind* and *degree* of forgiveness we ask from God by our exercise of mercy towards others. If he should forgive us only in *the same way* and to *the same extent* that we ever have forgiven, or ever can forgive, those who offend against us, we shall surely die in our sins. Christ himself gives us the key to the interpretation, when in the second deliverance of the prayer he teaches us to say, "Forgive us our sins, *for* we also forgive every one who is indebted to us." And the true force of "for" is explained in the familiar words of our Catechism: "We pray that God, for Christ's sake, would freely pardon all our sins, which we are the rather encouraged to ask, because by his grace we are enabled from the heart to forgive others." While, therefore, our forgiveness of others is neither the meritorious condition nor the measure of that divine forgiveness for which we pray, it is our *encouragement* in prayer; simply because it is the fruit and the evidence of our faith in Christ, and of the dominion of his grace in the soul. The words of CALVIN on this point are weighty and beautiful: "The forgiveness we ask from God does not *depend* on the forgiveness we grant to others; but the design of Christ was to exhort us, in this manner, to forgive the offences which have been committed against us, and, at the same time, to give, as it were, the impression of his seal to ratify the confidence in our own forgiveness. He intended to remind us of the feelings which we ought to cherish towards brethren, when we desire to be reconciled to God. And certainly, if the Spirit of God reigns in our hearts, every description of ill-will and revenge ought to be banished. The Spirit is the witness of our adoption; and therefore it is put down simply as a mark to distinguish the children of God from strangers."

This exposition accords not only with the teaching of Scripture, but with Christian experience. The penitent believer will always and naturally exercise a tenderness towards his fellow-sinners, just in proportion to his own sense of sin, and his trust in the merits of Christ as the ground of pardon. "Wherefore," says the Saviour, "if ye forgive not men their trespasses, neither will your heavenly Father forgive you." And why? Simply because your hardness and severity towards others prove that your heart never melted in true penitence and faith towards God, and that your prayer is only a form and a mockery. "But if ye forgive men their trespasses, your heavenly Father will forgive you;" because this is a proof that your soul is in a gracious state, and therefore it may be an encouragement to ask, and an argument by which to enforce your petition. You may come to your Father's mercy-seat, and, appealing to him as the searcher of hearts, may say, "I do now freely forgive every one who has trespassed against me, and, in view of this fruit of thy grace, lay a humble claim to that forgiveness thou hast promised to the penitent and believing soul."

What is the precise nature and extent of that forgiveness we are to exercise towards our fellow-sinners? Obviously the term "debtors" in the latter part of the petition must be interpreted consistently with its meaning in the first part. It does not refer chiefly, if at all, to those who are under pecuniary obligation to us, but to those who have offended us as we have offended God. It is also obvious that our forgiveness of such debtors does not signify merely the restraining of our resentment from violent outward expression, but the *removal* of all such resentment, and the cultivation of kind feelings even towards those who have injured us. We cannot forgive as God does. We cannot release our fellow-men from the guilt of their wrong-doing, even though we have been its chief object. But in some good, though imperfect degree, we can be, like our Father in heaven, free from wrath, revenge, and hatred; and we can imitate, in some measure, that infinite love which sends sunshine and rain upon the evil as well as the good.

Of course this does not forbid the enforcing

of public justice. Christian forgiveness has no affinity with that mawkish sympathy for criminals which makes the magistrate cease to be a terror to evil-doers. Such sympathy is cruel alike to the community and to the wretches it encourages in crime. Nor does a forgiving spirit forbid us to seek legal redress for our personal wrongs, when such redress can be obtained without doing greater injury than that we seek to remedy, and without indulgence of revengeful passions on our part. Neither, again, does a forgiving spirit forbid our profiting by past experience so as to avoid future trouble. The divine precept reads, " when ye stand praying, *forgive*." It is nowhere written forgive *and forget*. This human addition to the Saviour's commandment either means nothing beyond what he enjoins, or else its meaning is inconsistent with Christian prudence, and with the exercise of forgiveness itself. It is only when we remember an injury that we can fully and freely forgive it. If a man in whom we have confided betrays our confidence, injures our estate, stains our reputation, disturbs our domestic peace; while we abstain from all revenge and bitterness in our hearts towards him, and do him good if we have opportunity, the triumph of divine grace over our natural resentments is the more signal in proportion to the distinctness with which we remember and apprehend the wrong he has done us. It is, therefore, no impeachment of our sincerity in saying, "I forgive," if candor compels us to add, "I *cannot* forget." We *ought not* to forget, so as to give the betrayer of our confidence an opportunity to repeat his treachery. And yet in perfect harmony with this Christian prudence, and with the memory which is an essential part of our moral and intellectual being, we may — and, if we would enjoy God's favor, we must — cultivate a forgiving spirit. Such a spirit is inconsistent with that morbid sense of our own importance which is easily offended. Some minds are so sensitive that every shadow wounds them; so jealous that trifles light as a'r become weighty offences in their eyes; so ready to defend their real or fancied rights that every point of contact with the world inflicts a sense of injury; and thus their habit of feeling vibrates between antagonism and complaint. The spirit of forgiveness can find no repose in such a nest. And the spirit which forbids the harboring of evil suspicions is no less inconsistent with the cherishing of malice and revenge for real offences. There are occasions when we do well to be angry, but they are great trials to our Christian graces. A good man's anger, according to an old proverb, is like the spark which the steel strikes from the flint: it requires a hard blow to kindle it, and it soon expires. But how seldom is the truth of this saying verified! No fire is so easy to kindle and none so hard to extinguish as our human resentments. Even among those who worship at the same altar and break bread at the same table, how often are petty offences, which ought to have been buried the day they were born, nursed and magnified until they grow into giant evils!

The spirit of forgiveness forbids a hard and selfish prosecution of our worldly interests. Seeking redress for personal wrongs, by all lawful means, is a very different thing from the cold-blooded disregard for the feelings and welfare of others with which some men drive on the car of their own prosperity. This is the charge which stands in God's book against many a man, who boasts that he has built up his fortune by strict commercial integrity, and seeks to win the reputation of great liberality. He subscribes largely to schemes of Christian benevolence. He purposes in his heart, and perhaps announces publicly, that he means to leave the wealth he cannot carry with him to another world to found charitable institutions in this. And yet that same man, so liberal in intention to posterity, daily grinds the faces of the poor, and tramples on the misfortunes of his less successful competitors. His cold, keen eye never moistens at the sight of suffering, nor lights up with pleasure, except in the prospect of some grand speculation. The law of kindness is never on his tongue, except when he is striving to make a profitable bargain. He knows of no standard by which to measure a man except his ability to pay. He will exact the last penny and the last hour of toil from his debtors, in the spirit of the man in the parable, who took his fellow-servant by the throat, saying, "Pay me that thou owest." And he not only justifies, but glories in, this course, upon the plea that *business is business*, and charity entirely another matter; thus boastfully divorcing his daily life from the spirit of Christ and the obligations of the gospel. Can the man who lives six days in the week according to such principles consistently pray on the seventh, saying, " Forgive us our debts as we forgive our debtors " ?

Finally, a forgiving spirit forbids the exaggeration and needless repetition of another's faults. It is bad enough to behold the mote that is in our brother's eye, while we consider not the beam that is in our own. But it is still worse, when, instead of saying to him, " Brother, let me pull the mote out of thine eye," we employ ourselves in reporting and exaggerating it to others. If we could sit aloof and listen to the conversation of the world, even in its most refined and cultivated circles, we should be astonished to find how largely it is made up of the repetition of petty personal wrongs, which, though they amount to nothing in themselves, serve to inflame and irritate the mind of the narrator; or of indignant denunciation against persons of whose opinions and conduct the declaimer is entirely ignorant. It is easy for both men and women to form such a habit of evil speaking as will make its indulgence familiar and almost needful to their enjoyment as their daily bread. Some savage peoples are so depraved in their natural appetites as to relish the vilest food; and some, more civilized, eat up the sins of God's people, — yea, bite and devour one another's reputation. Let us remember that a forgiving spirit dwells not in the bosom of a talebearer or a backbiter; and, if we would cultivate that spirit, let us learn to bridle our tongue.

And yet, guard as we may against jealousy and malice, selfishness and evil-speaking, all our efforts will fail unless divine grace shall put the true spirit of forgiveness into our hearts. Let us pray that the Holy Ghost may dwell in us continually, convincing us of sin, leading us to the cross of Christ, and enabling us to imitate Him who, in his dying hour, prayed for his murderers. There is no place where the great lesson of forgiveness can be so effectually learned as at the mount of crucifixion. There we see the enormity of our own sins; and, if we are suitably humbled by the view, bitterness and wrath cannot abide in our souls. There, too, we see the bright pattern of the Saviour we profess to follow. The spirit of Christ, without which we are none of his, is the spirit of grace and supplications; and it embraces both friend and foe in its wide and gentle arms. "Father, forgive them: they know not what they do." May God enable us to drink deep of that spirit, and to show forth its beauty and its power in our daily life.

CHAPTER VII.

"And lead us not into Temptation, but deliver us from Evil."

EVERY step of our progress in the interpretation of this divine prayer brings out more clearly the correspondence between the written word of God and the record of a believer's experience. The one is the impress and the counterpart of the other. When he puts these petitions into the lips of his true disciples, the great High Priest of our profession gives utterance to the desire his own grace has kindled in their hearts. Thus the cry for daily bread, quickening in us the consciousness of all want, temporal and spiritual, leads naturally to the prayer for pardoning mercy, which constitutes our first great need as sinners under the condemnation of the law, and to the expression of that forgiving spirit towards others which always accompanies our sense of the divine forgiveness. But, if our Lord's prayer stopped here, it would be incomplete. There is a lower deep in the mystery of iniquity, and a more sublime height in the mystery of salvation, to both of which the true believer must attain. Christ came to save his people not only from the condemnation of sin, but from sin *itself;* from its power and pollution, as well as from its penal consequences. When the disciple has received the blessed assurance that his debt of everlasting punishment has been freely cancelled, and the sweet consciousness of divine mercy has expelled from his heart all wrath and bitterness toward those who have trespassed against him, he is still conscious of inherent sinfulness, of exposure to trials which in his own strength he can never endure, of an unfitness for the perfect fellowship of God's holy kingdom, which, of himself, he can never remove. Set free from the condemnation of the written law, he still " finds a law in his members warring against the law of his mind," and threatening in any unguarded moment to bring him into captivity to sin. His thirst after righteousness is not yet satisfied. That clean heart and that right spirit, in which the kingdom of grace comes to its consummation in glory, are not yet fully

THE MODEL PRAYER. 147

created and renewed within him. Innumerable enemies still compass him about. His godly sorrow for past sin deepens and perpetuates itself in a godly fear of future transgressions, and extorts from him, as it did from the apostle, the pathetic exclamation, " Wretched man that I am, who shall deliver me!" At this stage of Christian experience, the petition before us comes in, to interpret our desires and to teach us how they may be realized. The Captain of our salvation, who, not only by his divine knowledge but by his human experience also, has threaded every labyrinth of sin, and come off more than conqueror over every form of evil, instructs us by example and by precept to seek deliverance in prayer. We are to arm and encourage ourselves for the conflict by invoking the aid of our almighty Father, saying, " Lead us not into temptation, but deliver us from evil."

And it is in this nice adaptation of the petition before us to Christian experience, as illustrated in other Scriptures, that we find the true solution of several difficulties which have been suggested in regard to its interpretation. For example, some have insisted that this petition ought to be separated into two; so that the latter clause, "but deliver us from evil," shall constitute a seventh petition, distinct from the preceding six. The formularies of the Lutheran Church recognize this distinction. Augustine, and many writers since his day, defend it upon what seems to us the fanciful ground " that throughout all Scripture seven is the covenant number, the number of sacrifice and the number of prayer, the signature of all meetings between God and man."* Admitting, what seems to be doubtful, that the grammatical structure of the words will bear such a division, and conceding that the particle *but* does not expressly indicate an antithetical and positive presentation in the latter clause of the same idea which is negatively expressed in the former, we still think that Christian experience, as expounded in other Scriptures, must accept the two parts of the petition as parallel and essentially synonymous expressions of the same desire. It is both a doctrine of Scripture and an experimental fact that we must be exposed to temptation and liable to fall into it, so long as we are in any wise under the dominion of evil. And it is furthermore a doctrine of experience that evil is present with us so long as

* Trench.

THE MODEL PRAYER. 149

we are in the flesh. And, therefore, when we pray, "lead us not into temptation," an intelligent perception of that which gives temptation all its power suggests the more positive and comprehensive form of the same petition, "deliver us from evil." Though the two ideas are distinct, they are essential parts of one and the same experience. The realization of the one necessarily involves the fulfilment of the other. A Christian can never be free from liability to fall into temptation until he is finally and fully delivered from all evil. And this leads us to explain more fully what we have already assumed, the distinction between a mere exposure to temptation and being *led into it*. When the Saviour says, "Watch and pray, that ye enter not into temptation," he surely does not mean that by watchfulness and prayer we can bring ourselves into such a position that we shall *never be tempted*. This would be to make our worldly estate superior to that of Christ himself; to multiply and make void a multitude of precepts which direct us how to resist and overcome evil; to abrogate a multitude of promises which proclaim the blessedness of the man who endures temptation. By *entering* or *being led into* temptation is evidently meant coming under and yielding to its power; so that, instead of being delivered from evil, we shall be overcome by it, and subjected to its pollution and control.

And here another difficulty occurs, about which there has been much discussion. What is the precise meaning of "evil" in the latter clause of the petition? The interpretation turns upon the question whether the original word (τοῦ πονηροῦ) is to be taken as masculine or neuter. If masculine, it signifies the Evil *One*; *i.e.*, the *Devil*. If neuter, it signifies evil in general; *i.e.*, *all sin*. Our translators, and the general consent of all Christians from the beginning, have taken it in the latter sense. That this is the true sense, we are satisfied, aside from other reasons, by the consideration that it is the more comprehensive, and better adapted to Christian experience. We do not exclude, but include the Evil *One*, in our desire to be free from evil. We know that he is the great tempter, that he is the prince of this world, that he rules in the children of disobedience. We know, also, that "whosoever sinneth is of the Devil," assimilated to him in character and conduct just so far as his indulgence in sin extends. And, furthermore, we know that sin brings us under the power of the Devil; and that as he is the great tempter in this world, so also, of those that are unforgiven, he will be the great punisher in the world to come. But while we accept, with a literal faith, all the Bible teaches about the Evil One, we know also from Scripture and experience that he is not the only tempter. There are sins in which he has no part; sins to which we are led aside and enticed by our own lust; sins by which we tempt Satan to tempt us, and without which he could have no power at all over us. When, therefore, we come, under the pressure of our trials and with the consciousness of our weakness, to the mercy-seat, we do not deceive ourselves by praying simply to be delivered from the Evil One, as though he were our only or our worst enemy; but, including his assaults among our other temptations, we offer the comprehensive petition to be delivered from all sin, — whether the provocation to commit it comes from the world in which we live, from the spiritual wickedness with which we wrestle, or from our own hearts, out of which proceed all manner of evil.

Yet another and still more intricate question which demands solution refers to the meaning of the word "temptation." In its primary and most common acceptation, it signifies *a solicitation to sin.* But can the word be used in this sense in the Lord's prayer? Can we ask God not to lead us into temptation, meaning thereby that he should not lead us to yield to the solicitations of evil? To this question many hastily answer in the negative, and confirm their answer by the Scripture which says, " God is not tempted of evil, neither tempteth he any man." They therefore seek for another meaning to the word "temptation," and find it in those passages of Scripture in which *afflictions* are called *temptations;* *i.e.*, trials, or tests of character. As, for example, in the record where it is said, " God did *tempt* Abraham ;" that is, he put the patriarch to the test of experiment, by commanding him to offer Isaac as a sacrifice upon the altar, intending thereby only to bring out and exhibit the faith and obedience of the father of the faithful. In the same way, as we are taught in many Scriptures, confirmed by our own experience, God tries the faith of all his children, as gold is tried in the fire. But we cannot accept this as the full explanation of the Saviour's meaning in the petition before us, for two obvious reasons: *First*, because afflictions as trials of our faith are part of God's uniform discipline, from which we have no warrant, and ought to have no desire, to ask for exemption. To offer such a prayer is equivalent to asking that he will disown us. "For if we be without chastening, whereof all are partakers, then are we bastards, and not sons." In this sense of the word, we ought rather to "count it all joy when we fall into divers temptations." *Secondly*, such an interpretation cuts the very heart out of the petition our Lord has taught us, and destroys its adaptation to our religious experience. What Christian can satisfy himself at the mercy-seat by merely asking not to be led into outward affliction? Even if it were proper to offer such a request, who could be content to omit all supplication in regard to those direct solicitations to sin to which we are ever exposed from within and from without? Who of us does not know by experience that we never can be delivered from evil until we are completely free from liability to fall under temptation, in the common sense of the word? And who of us does not know instinctively that only the almighty God can secure us against that liability?

If it be said, in response, that the afflictions God sends upon us for the trial of our faith may, through our weakness, become occasions for sin, and therefore we may properly pray not to be led in this way into temptation, we reply again that, while this is true, it still leaves out of the account and excludes from our prayer those innumerable solicitations to sin which come to us through our prosperity, through the lusts of our own hearts, and through the power of Satan. And besides, if afflictions are to be regarded and deprecated in this petition simply as occasions and inducements to sin, the explanation does not remove the original difficulty. If God sends a trial upon us, knowing in his divine omniscience that the sorrow it inflicts will overwhelm and lead us into unbelief, rebellion, or any other sin, the question in regard to his *leading us into temptation* is not solved, but only removed one step further back. There it stands; and it cannot be put aside by any metaphysical subtlety. The Saviour teaches us to pray, " Lead us not into temptation;" and temptation, as every Christian knows, is here used in a comprehensive sense, to signify whatever may cause us to sin. The true solution of this and all similar difficulties is found not in any abstract reasoning, but in the simple-hearted faith which regards God as an absolute sovereign, and looks up through all secondary causes to him as the supreme arbiter of all events. Thus Job, when he was robbed by the Chaldeans and Sabeans, said, " The Lord hath taken away." It never occurred to the patriarch that his simple and sublime faith in God's absolute sovereignty over the conduct of wicked men made him a participant in their wickedness, or impaired in any way their responsibility for their own evil actions. In the same manner that God took away the oxen and the camels of Job through the voluntary evil doings of the Sabean and Chaldean robbers, he leads into temptation those whom the world, the flesh, and the Devil induce to sin. All through the Scriptures, *God is said to do that which he permits to be done.* And this form of expression is used not as a mere figure of speech. It covers the profound and glorious truth that his permission is not the result of ignorance or impotency; that he permits sin, and whatever leads to its commission, not because he cannot prevent it, but in the exercise of his infinite wisdom and with a view to the accomplishment of his own ulterior designs. We may not be able fully to reconcile the Scriptures which assert this profound doctrine with the declaration that he is not tempted of evil, neither tempteth any man; but faith accepts both as equally true. We know that men are free within the sphere of their own moral agency; but we know also that God is supreme over all, and worketh all things after the counsel of his own will. A creature's freedom is a wheel within a wheel, a circle circumscribed by divine wisdom and omnipotence.

Perhaps the most accurate paraphrase of the petition we are considering would be, "*Permit us not to be led* into temptation." And yet we do not dare, after the example of some of the Christian Fathers, to substitute this human explanation for the words Christ has taught us. Doubtless he himself knew what he would do, when he instructed us to say, "Lead us not into temptation;" and we think one obvious design was to humble us at the mercy-seat with a sense of our inability to comprehend the mystery of God's providence, and at the same time to encourage us with the thought that all things, even our manifold temptations, are under his absolute control. That we may

THE MODEL PRAYER. 157

be the better prepared to lay hold upon this encouragement, let us take a brief survey of the temptations to which we are exposed. (1) Like the Saviour who was tempted in all points as we are, we are exposed to the assaults and wiles of the Devil. The existence and agency of this Evil One are as plainly revealed in the Bible as the being of God. The titles bestowed upon him indicate his character and influence. He is *Satan*, the adversary; the *Devil*, one who sets others at variance; a slanderer or false accuser; the father of lies; the prince of the power of the air; the prince of devils; the spirit that worketh in the children of disobedience; the *Tempter*. The history of his apostasy from God, and of his evil agency in the world, is plainly written that we may not be ignorant of his devices. He is that Old Serpent who tempted Eve (Rev. xii. 9, 2 Cor. xi. 3); and from the days of Eden, through every age, " he deceiveth the whole world," and " goeth about like a roaring lion, seeking whom he may devour." The rash speculation which would make all these Scriptures mean nothing more than the evil that is in man's own heart is sufficiently refuted by the simple record that " Jesus was led up of the Spirit into the wilderness to be tempted of the Devil." Who was it that tempted Christ? The evil in his own heart! How then was he " holy, and harmless, and separate from sinners "? and how could he truthfully say, " The prince of this world cometh, and hath nothing in me "? The Christian who is accustomed to watch his own heart has no difficulty in the literal acceptance of the Scripture testimony on this awful subject. He has thoughts and emotions which he knows are not self-originated. They come unbidden, and remain in spite of his strenuous efforts to expel them. In the most sacred places, in the hour of sweetest communion with God and heavenly things, his mind is suddenly filled with feelings and imaginations which are repulsive to all his cherished principles, and against whose entrance he fights with his utmost strength. In times of affliction, when he would be still under the mighty hand of God, and bring his will into sweet subjection to the divine wisdom and love, a malicious and mighty spirit whispers thoughts of rebellion and blasphemy into his ear, and torments him with horrible suggestions of atheism and self-destruction. In days of prosperity, when he would fain retain a humble sense of his dependence on the great Benefactor, the same evil spirit suggests thoughts of pride and self-sufficiency. Sneer and speculate as you may, O Infidel! the Christian knows there is such a being as the Tempter. He knows it by a consciousness deeper and broader than all the discourses of reason. We hear his horrible suggestions, we feel his hot breath fanning the embers of passion and lust in our hearts, we smart under his fiery darts coming swiftly and rankling sorely in our souls. He may not be thus manifest to you, simply because you have never renounced his dominion, nor strenuously resisted his devices. Floating down the stream before the current and the breeze, a man does not realize the force of the wind and tide. But let him reverse his course, and he shall find the need of plying his oars with diligence and strength. Let a sinner, who has long floated down toward the gulf of black despair, lulled into carnal security by the very power which drives him on to destruction, begin to steer heavenward, and he will soon learn by experience that the kingdom of God requireth violence. The Evil One is not most busy with the careless and ungodly. His mightiest assault was against the Son of God; and the violence of his temptations against men is always proportioned to their nearness to the Saviour.

(2) But while we thus insist upon the reality of Satan's temptations, let it not be forgotten that his success depends upon our own inward lusts and corruptions. In the work of temptation, the Evil One is confederate with our evil heart. Every man has within him by nature the seeds and motives of all sin. "From within, out of the heart of men, proceed evil thoughts, adulteries, fornications, murders, thefts, covetousness, wickedness, deceit, lasciviousness, an evil eye, blasphemy, pride, foolishness; all these evil things come from within, and defile a man." These elements of evil may be variously combined: they may be concealed from a man's own observation by many excellent traits of character; they may be partially subdued and kept under by the power of divine grace; but, however concealed and mortified, deceitfulness above all things, and desperate wickedness, are characteristics of the universal heart of man. The popular idea of outward wickedness, combined with a good heart, is a mere fiction. Every man's heart is the worst part of him. Satan well knows how to adapt his temptations

to the peculiarities of human character. With keen penetration he discerns the weak points, and with cunning skill adjusts the time and instruments of his attacks. He who would resist temptation must keep his own heart with all diligence ; as a wise general keeps the fortress that is not only assaulted by enemies without, but constantly liable to be betrayed by traitors within. For, however great may be the power and subtlety of the Evil One, he is not almighty: he cannot force the human will, nor prevail over us without our own consent. When a man is led into temptation, " he is drawn away of his own lust, and enticed." And, alas ! this very freedom, of which men are so apt to boast, is the chief source of our danger ; for the heart is *prone*, it leans over, to evil. How much easier is it to yield to sinful solicitations than to resist them ! What a little spark of provocation will inflame the soul with lust or pride ! How small a prospect of gain, or sensual indulgence will suffice to make us pause, and even turn aside from the straight and rugged path of duty ! It is an experimental truth that the course of nature inclines downward, and that Satan with his temptations is rowing with the wind and tide in his favor.

(3) Moreover, this confederation of the Evil One with the evil heart is strengthened by the evil world in which we live, — a world where Satan's seat is, and whose friendship is enmity with God. By the "world" the Bible means either those wicked men whom Satan uses as his agents to resist the triumph of genuine religion, or those outward circumstances which, though neither good nor evil in themselves, afford opportunities for the Tempter to carry on his work. The Saviour used the word in the former sense, when he said, " If the world hate you, ye know that it hated me before it hated you. If ye were of the world, the world would love his own ; but because ye are not of the world, but I have chosen you out of the world, therefore the world hateth you. Remember the word that I spake unto you, The servant is not greater than his lord. If they have persecuted me, they will also persecute you." These words are as true to-day as when they fell from the Master's lips. Men of loose principles and wicked lives hate vital piety. Both the profession and the practice of a Christian are a standing rebuke to their ungodliness. And because they feel and smart under that rebuke, they are ever ready to rave

THE MODEL PRAYER. 163

and rail at what they call the fanaticism or the hypocrisy of the man of God; ever ready to believe and propagate a scandalous report against him; to entice him into some sinful indulgence, and then go abroad and publish his shame. The records of eternity alone will reveal how much of temptation and persecution are endured in private by the followers of Christ. How often does the Christian find his foes among them of his own household! How hard it is to stand firm against the oppositions, the scoffs, and the allurements of near and dear friends! and how difficult, especially for the young disciple, to resist the subtle reasonings and importunities of companions, who would seduce him from his integrity, so that his firmness may no longer be a living reproach against their evil courses!

But by the "world" the Scriptures mean not only evil men, who thus lend themselves to do the meanest work of the Devil: the outward circumstances of the Christian, though morally indifferent in themselves, afford opportunities and occasions for Satan's temptations, and for the development of the heart's natural lusts. Every occupation and position in life has its peculiar dangers; and even lawful pleasures and possessions may be perverted into a snare. If we are in adverse circumstances, envy and discontent seek to pour their bitter waters into the soul; and if prosperity crowns our efforts, the " bright day that brings the adder forth " quickens the lust of the flesh, and the lust of the eye, and the pride of life. How often does a change in worldly circumstances seem utterly to transform the character of a man! In a low and obscure estate he appears to be sincere and humble-minded. But clothe him with a little brief authority, give him the dignity and emoluments of office, let riches increase and his social position be exalted, and behold how he swells! Pride covers him as with a garment, and he carelessly commits the sins from which he once turned with abhorrence. From another who has always been surrounded with the good things of life, and whose good-humored self-possession seemed to qualify him for his station, let riches and social influence be taken away, and how the milk of human kindness curdles within him, until his heart and mouth are filled with wrath and bitterness! There is no one thing in regard to which we are more frequently self-deceived than in the supposition of what we would do if we were in other men's circumstances. The traveller, when he looks up to some distant mountain, sees only the green foliage on its sides, the light that plays in beauty on its summit, and the still firmament that sheds down upon the scene the reflected hues of heaven. But when he comes to the actual ascent, he finds new rocks and pitfalls at every step; and ere he gains the coveted elevation, his hand is too weary to grasp, and his eye too dim to behold, the coveted glory, — even if the enchanted vision had not faded at his approach. Thus, in the great journey of life, the things which seem most enticing in the distance develop new trials at every stage of its progress; and when the eager aspirant has attained to that charmed circle of fashion and ease and social distinction which claims to be pre-eminently the world, if the enthusiasm of earlier years has not already evaporated in the struggle, he soon finds that fulness begets satiety, and the care of riches chokes the remembrance and the enjoyment of God our maker.

Such is a brief survey of the temptations to which we are exposed. Oh, when we contemplate this array of evils, — this triple combination of Satan, the world, and our own hearts, all working together to betray us into sin, and drag us back from the pathway to heaven, — does it not seem impossible to be saved? Blessed be God! there is one weapon before which Apollyon and his host will always flee, — one calm and sure retreat, where we may find refuge from the world, and where even the tumults of our own heart may be stilled.

> "Ah! whither could we flee for aid,
> When tempted, desolate, dismayed, —
> Or how the hosts of hell defeat, —
> Had suffering saints no mercy-seat?"

"He that trusteth in his own heart is a fool." The history of the saints unites with our own experience to confirm the proverb. Peter and David and Noah and Lot and Adam trusted in themselves, and fell. Let us take warning from their example, and abide under the shadow of the Almighty.

"The Lord knoweth how to deliver the godly out of temptations." There are two ways in which our prayers may be answered: first, by keeping us from such assaults of temptation as would prove overwhelming; and, second, by sustaining us in such as do come upon us. God is able to bind Satan, and entirely restrain his power. He is greater than our hearts, and by a single exercise of his almighty grace could utterly subdue their lusts. The world is under his absolute control, and he could so arrange its affairs that it should present to our experience no occasion for trial. All this he has promised ultimately to do. And when his exceeding great and precious promises shall be fulfilled, the circle of prayer will be complete, the first petition will swallow up the last, and the final coming of the kingdom of glory will secure our deliverance from all evil. But, meanwhile, our Lord delayeth his coming; and the time seems long to those who for "a season must needs be in heaviness through manifold temptations." We grow weary of the conflict with the Adversary. We are ready to cry out, How long, O Lord, how long shall Satan buffet me, and the world lead me astray from thee, and my own heart betray me into sin? Have patience, O tempted soul! God's plan is best. Better to be thus exposed to trial, and finally enjoy the deliverance and the triumph, than never to have known the hour and power of darkness. Over the furnace sits the Refiner, watching the process, directing its issues, and ready to arrest it when the end is accomplished. This promise stands sure: "God is faithful, who will not suffer you to be tempted above that ye are able; but will with the temptation also make a way of escape, that ye may be able to bear it." Look at the record in which his faithfulness is demonstrated. The Bible history is full of illustrations; and so are the memorials laid up in our own experience. Look back over the history of your life: the way is studded with Ebenezers and stones of memorial. If you had been told at the outset all the trials that were appointed for you, you could not have endured the anticipation. And yet, as the successive conflicts came, you conquered in them. Though you have often been cast down, you have never been destroyed. Many a lion, before which you trembled at a distance, has been found chained when you approached. Many a deep sea of troubles has divided before you at the touch of a rod mightier than that of Moses. Many a stormy passion has subsided at the voice of Him who speaks to the winds and waves, and they obey him. "His grace has kept you till this day." Let the experience of the past encourage you to pray, and to believe that "grace will bring you home." God is able to deliver from evil, else you and I would long since have made shipwreck of our faith. Let us still dwell in the secret place of the Most High, and shut the doors about us till the indignation be overpast. Let us trust in the divine sovereignty, and pray, " Lead us not into temptation," until this mystery of iniquity is dissolved in the light of His presence who will shortly tread Satan under our feet, and the same voice which summons us from the conflict to the crown proclaims our perfect and everlasting deliverance from evil.

And if for this continuance in prayer and faith we need any further encouragement, we may find it in the earthly triumph of Him who was tempted in all points as we are, without sin, — linked as it is with his living intercession in heaven for them that are tempted. In the hour of trial, study the history of Christ's conflict in the wilderness. It is a blessed history, not only as an example of the way to resist temptation with the sure weapon of the word of God, but because it gives us also the sure pledge of our ultimate victory. As our advocate and mediator, he went into that contest, and came off more than conqueror;

and now he speaks to us from the holy place of intercession, saying, "Satan hath desired to have thee, that he may sift thee as wheat; but I have prayed for thee, that thy faith fail not." While we pray for ourselves, what mighty intercessions are those which Christ offers for us in heaven! They come from a heart deeply experienced in all our trials. Let us therefore come boldly to the throne of grace. For while we pray " Lead us not into temptation," the great High Priest understands and feels that petition as no other being can ; and as he repeats it for us before the mercy-seat, it is purified and perfumed by the power of a divine yet human sympathy.

CHAPTER VIII.

"*For Thine is the Kingdom, and the Power, and the Glory, for ever.*"

THERE is an open controversy among the learned as to the genuineness of these words. Many critical commentators maintain that they were not uttered by the Saviour, nor written by the Evangelist in the original record of his instructions. In the best modern editions of the Greek Testament they are either omitted entirely, or placed in brackets to signify that their right to be retained is questionable. But Biblical criticism has not banished the passage from the lips and hearts of Christians, nor lessened to any considerable extent the faith of the Church in its inspiration as an integral part of the Lord's prayer. Nor are the critics entirely agreed among themselves. We shall not undertake to cite authorities, nor to rehearse at length the arguments on either side of the question. As to the objections to the genuineness of the passage, it will be sufficient to observe that they are chiefly *external* and *negative ;* being based upon the omission of the words from many records, where, if genuine, we would naturally expect to find them. They are not found in the Latin version of the Bible, commonly called the Vulgate, which, from a very early period, has been regarded as authoritative in the Church of Rome ; nor in the writings of Tertullian, Cyprian, Jerome, and Augustine, all of whom wrote comments on the Lord's prayer; nor in some of the most ancient Greek manuscripts out of which our present New Testament is collated. Those who regard these omissions as conclusive proof that the passage was not found in the Gospel as originally written by Matthew account for its presence in other manuscripts, in the writings of some of the Greek Fathers, and especially in the Syriac version of the New Testament, which is probably the oldest translation in existence, by supposing that it was gradually "interpolated from the ancient liturgies in which we know it formed the response of the people, the

prayer alone being pronounced by the priest."*
ALFORD, and others among the most eminent
critics, maintain this opinion. To the objection
that the Greek Church never would have presumed to add, from their liturgies, to a form
of prayer delivered by Christ himself, these
critics answer that they never did *formally*
add it, the doxology being introduced gradually, and, no doubt, at first written in a different character, and in red ink, and in the
margin, as found in several manuscripts. On
the other hand, many writers, such as CALVIN, — and especially the learned Dr. Witsius,
whose work on the Lord's prayer has long been
considered a standard, — contend with great
earnestness for the genuineness of the passage. They insist that its omission from some
ancient manuscripts is no conclusive argument
that it is improperly written in others of
equally high antiquity; that its exclusion from
the Latin Vulgate is no satisfactory proof that
it should be regarded as spurious in the Syriac
version, which is confessedly of older date;
that the silence of Tertullian, Cyprian, and
Augustine, who did not find it in their Latin
editions, is not sufficient to set aside the testi-

* Bloomfield.

mony of Chrysostom and other Greek Fathers, who wrote at an earlier period, and "drew from the fountains, while the others drew from the streams;" that it is far more probable that the Greek Fathers learned it *from* the Gospel than that it found its way from their writings or from their liturgies *into* the sacred Scriptures. As to the omission of it from the record in Luke's Gospel, it is considered sufficient to observe, that the Lord's prayer, as there written, was delivered on a different occasion, and varies in other points from the record in Matthew. It is well said that "no argument against any narrative can be founded on the silence of a single evangelist; what is wholly or partly omitted by one must be supplied from the writings of another." Indeed the argument from Luke's omission has been skilfully turned into a proof for the genuineness of the words as found in Matthew. For, if the passage is interpolated in Matthew, it is not easy to see why it has been left out of Luke, as it would have been as easy to introduce it in the one place as in the other. Its presence in the former Gospel and its absence in the latter seem rather to prove it genuine.

Without undertaking positively to decide

the dispute, in which we have given this brief summary of arguments on either side, we think every candid mind will admit that the *external* objections to the genuineness of the passage are not absolutely conclusive, and that modern critics take too much upon themselves when they strike it authoritatively from the sacred text. And now, if, giving it the full benefit of this doubt, we turn to the *internal* evidence of the passage, the argument seems to be altogether in favor of its genuineness. Some indeed have contended that this doxology only mars the beauty and completeness of the prayer; but their views on this point are evidently suggested by their zeal to maintain the conclusions of their external criticism. The heart of God's people and the analogy of the faith are both against them. The doxology has maintained its place in the prayers of the whole Christian Church, in our English version of the Bible, and in the standards of all Protestant denominations, in spite of all the historic arguments adduced against it, because it is suitable to Christian consciousness and experience and to the teaching of all Scripture. We do not admit, with STEIR, that here or anywhere " internal criticism ought to maintain its prerogative over the external testimonies of the manuscripts;" but, where the testimony of the manuscripts is ambiguous and doubtful, we certainly think that the instincts of the Christian heart, and especially the analogy of other Scriptures may properly come in to turn the scale. If this doxology is an uninspired addition to the sacred text, it is certainly the most cunning and successful interpolation ever attempted. It fits like a crown upon the whole prayer; it sums up all the petitions and turns them into praise; it completes the circle of our devout desires, bringing them back to the source from whence they start, in the kingdom and power of our Father in heaven; it sums up both the argument and the end of all prayer in the glory of God; and it seals what goes before with our desire and expectation to be heard, in the solemn *Amen*. In all this, it not only interprets the devout believer's experience, but epitomizes the testimony and example of other Scriptures. The authority for using such doxologies does not depend on this single passage. Similar ascriptions abound in the Bible. A very striking example is found in the prayer of David, recorded in 1 Chron. xxix. 10-13: —

THE MODEL PRAYER. 177

Wherefore David blessed the Lord before all the congregation: and David said, Blessed be thou, Lord God of Israel our Father, for ever and ever.

Thine, O Lord, is the greatness, and the power, and the glory, and the victory, and the majesty: for all that is in the heaven and in the earth is thine; thine is the kingdom, O Lord, and thou art exalted as head above all.

Both riches and honor come of thee, and thou reignest over all; and in thy hand is power and might; and in thy hand it is to make great, and to give strength unto all.

Now therefore, our God, we thank thee, and praise thy glorious name.

The conclusion of the Lord's prayer is but a condensed statement of these words and sentiments. The inspired apostles frequently use language embodying the same spirit, and strikingly analogous in its form. Thus Paul in 1 Tim. i. 17: "Now unto the King eternal, immortal and invisible, the only wise God, be honor and glory for ever and ever. *Amen.*"

So also Jude concludes his epistle with these words: "To the only wise God our Saviour be glory and majesty, dominion and power, both now and ever. *Amen.*" The worship of heaven, of which we catch glorious glimpses in the book of Revelation, abounds in such doxologies; and it is part of our preparation for the service and enjoyment of that blessed world to conclude and crown all our petitions here with the intelligent and hearty ascription, " Thine is the kingdom, and the power, and the glory, for ever. Amen." Nor are these words to be regarded as a mere doxological outburst of feeling, by which we are allied in sympathy and prepared for fellowship with glorified saints. They have another aspect, which, if not so ecstatic, is no less full of comfort for us, in this world, where petitions for pardon, support and deliverance mingle with our ascriptions of praise: they express the ground of hope on which all our petitions are based, and teach us that the success of prayer depends on God alone, and not upon our imperfect merits.

Let us therefore meditate upon this conclusion of our Lord's prayer: FIRST, as a DOXOLOGY or ASCRIPTION of PRAISE; and, SECONDLY, as an ARGUMENT in prayer.

The Lord's prayer begins and ends in the same point, forming, as it were, a circle, within which all our desires and supplications should move. The divine glory is the Alpha and the Omega. The first petition expresses our desire that our heavenly Father's name may be hallowed; and, after embracing in the subsequent petitions all our wants for time and eternity, we turn back in the partial, but blessed fulfilment of our own prayer, to hallow our Father's name in this sublime doxology; anticipating the time when evil, temptation, guilt, and want shall all be done away, and there shall remain on earth, as in heaven, naught but everlasting praise.

From this example we may learn the nature of praise. It is the expression of devout emotions excited in a believer's heart by the contemplation of God's character and works. It includes thanksgiving, or the utterance of gratitude in remembrance of what he has done for us; and adoration, or the expression of awe, wonder, and delight in view of his glorious attributes. It must always consist of two parts, an inward emotion and an outward expression, — the feeling of the heart and the language of the lips. There is no such thing as dumb praise. Both heart and tongue must be partners in the work. Speech was given to us for the very purpose of expressing the gratitude and adoration of the soul. How beautiful are the Psalmist's words: "Thou hast girded me with gladness; to the end that my glory may sing praise to thee, and not be silent." " Therefore my heart is glad, and my glory rejoiceth." "Awake up, my glory; awake psaltery and harp." The sweet singer of Israel calls his tongue his *glory*, the crowning excellence of his nature, because it gives utterance to the apprehensions of the understanding and the emotions of the heart towards God. He resolves to consecrate the divine gift of speech to the worship of the glorious Giver. "His praise shall be continually in my mouth." He desires to unite the hearts and voices of all saints in this delightful employment. "O come, let us sing unto the Lord: let us make a joyful noise to the Rock of our salvation. Let us come before his presence with thanksgiving, and make a joyful noise unto him with psalms. Sing unto the Lord, bless his name; shew forth his salvation from day to day. Declare his glory among the heathen, his wonders among all people." He would enlist all intelligent creatures in this blessed work. "Let every thing that hath breath praise the Lord." He would subsidize the concord of all sweet sounds to aid and emphasize the intelligent expression of the grateful and adoring heart. "Praise him with the sound of the trumpet; praise him with the psaltery and harp; praise him with stringed instruments and organs." In

THE MODEL PRAYER. 181

the sublime ardor of his devotion, he would enlist all inanimate objects, and harmonize every voice in nature in the universal anthem of praise. "Let the heavens rejoice, and the earth be glad; let the sea roar, and the fulness thereof; let the floods clap their hands; let the hills be joyful together, and all the trees of the wood rejoice." We cannot see how those who regard the Scriptures as the rule of all acceptable worship, and especially how those who insist upon restricting the service of song to the strict use of the Psalms of David, can consistently object to the aids of instrumental music in the singing of God's praise. The use of such instruments was sanctioned by divine authority in the worship of the temple; it is embalmed in those inspired odes which are the models of devotion in the Church of all ages; and the glimpses of heaven given to us in the last book of Revelation show us, that in the worship of glorified saints before the throne,

"Ten thousand harps and voices
Sound the notes of jubilee."

But let it be remembered that God is not praised by mere sound, however musical. The sound is desirable and sufferable, only so far as it helps the expression of the sense, and the sense must always centre in God himself. We are to praise him for his mighty acts, and according to his excellent greatness. We are solemnly to repeat his glorious titles, to rehearse his wondrous works, to extol his infinite attributes, to proclaim the memory of his bountiful dealings, to repeat the catalogue of all his benefits. We are to think of the myriad of worlds scattered through boundless space; the myriads of creatures in heaven, earth, and hell; and the unnumbered myriads more, which, for aught we know, may people the universe beyond the reach of our vision and the scope of his revelation: and with our souls dilated upon the sublime contemplation, we are to say, "Thine is the kingdom; thy throne is established in heaven, and thy dominion ruleth over all." We are to think of the might by which every fixed star is held in its place, and every planet guided in its orbit, and the world itself "hung upon nothing" in the midst of the well-ordered universe; of the strength that fixes the mountains and bounds the seas, and revolves the seasons in their beautiful vicissitude, and mixes the elements of seed-time and harvest in their secret laboratories, that the wants of every living thing may be supplied; of the strength that turns the hearts of men as the rivers of water; that stilleth the noise of the sea and the tumults of the people, and leaves the finger mark of divine control upon every page of history; and, above all, of the strength by which the human soul is redeemed, regenerated, and made holy, which the apostle calls " the exceeding greatness of his power to us-ward who believe:" and when by such contemplations we have filled our souls with wonder and gratitude, we are to look up to our Father's throne and say, "Thine is the power." We are to trace out the evidences of the Godhead in the things which are made; the divine attributes illustrated in the providence that sustains them; the wisdom and the grace revealed in the whole scheme of redemption; the justice that shall flame for evermore in the abode of the lost, and the love and mercy that will swell the everlasting songs of the ransomed in heaven: and with hearts all glowing, and tongues set on fire with the lofty theme, we are to crown our prayers and praises with the ascription, " Thine is the glory."

And when we have thus contemplated and

rehearsed the kingdom, power, and glory of God, which was, and is, and is to come, we are to sum up and express all our desires in regard to them, in the solemn AMEN, — *so let it be!*

Such praises, whether uttered in ecstatic anthems, with the mingled harmonies of harps and trumpets, in the general assembly of the firstborn in heaven; or in the choral symphonies of the multitude, who crowd Zion's gate on earth; or in the broken accents of the humblest child who prays to its Father in secret; come up as sweet incense before his throne, and call down his choicest blessing. For " whoso uttereth praise glorifieth God; " and they that glorify him shall enjoy him for ever.

Our obligation thus to praise God is infinite as his own nature, boundless as his lovingkindness and his wonderful works towards the children of men. It is based upon his own intrinsic excellence. He is the embodiment of every conceivable perfection. The universe is beautiful and majestic with the garniture of his skill and the reflection of his thoughts; but he is beauty and majesty themselves. Man, made in his image, has found out many inventions and done many wonderful things;

but He is the infinite source of all being, the substance of all wisdom, the essence of all power. In the outgoings of his being, the light is his shadow, and the stars the dust of his chariot-wheels. All the beauty of the heavens and the earth, all the discoveries of science, all the productions of genius, are but feeble streams and struggling rays: he is the infinite fountain, the eternal sun. For God is light; God is love; God is an infinite, eternal, and unchangeable spirit. Oh, is it not strange and horrible that, amid all the songs of the world, and all the eulogies that fill the hearts and lips of men, the name that is above every name, and the glory that shines beyond and above the heavens, should be so seldom and so feebly mentioned in words of adoration and praise?

Moreover, our obligation to praise God proceeds from our relations to him. Shall not our Creator, our Preserver, our Redeemer, our Father in heaven, receive some tribute from the creatures, some grateful acknowledgment from the children, upon whom he has lavished his bounty, and for whom he offered his only begotten Son in sacrifice? Oh, the meanness and enormity of forgetting him, when all he asks is our gratitude and adoration, finding their appropriate expression in words of praise! "Hear, O heavens, and give ear, O earth: for the Lord hath spoken, I have nourished and brought up children, and they have rebelled against me. The ox knoweth his owner, and the ass his master's crib: but Israel doth not know, my people doth not consider."

And, furthermore, our obligation is founded upon the influence of praise upon our own character and welfare. In his condescending love, this is one chief reason why it is required. Praise is comely for the upright, and it is a good thing to give thanks. God, in his infinite sufficiency for himself, does not need the tribute of any creature. Angels, with their veiled faces and their holy ascriptions, are not necessary to his happiness and glory. He was blessed for evermore, before they were created; he would be the ever-living God, were all the nations dead. But those heavenly hosts find their delight and their sustenance in praise. And surely it is a good thing for our own sake to emulate their fervid zeal. It exalts and purifies the soul to look from created things to their glorious Maker, from the imperfect earthly images to the brightness of the Father's glory, from the fleeting and sin-stained occupations of men to the everlasting fellowship and employments of saints and angels. No scene is so much like heaven as the assembly where hearts and voice blend in praise; and never are we doing so much to tune our souls for the worship of that temple where the Lord God giveth them light, as when we say sincerely, "Thine is the kingdom, and the power, and the glory."

Let us now briefly consider these words as an ARGUMENT in PRAYER.

It is one of the wonderful proofs of our heavenly Father's love that he permits and invites us to argue our case before him; saying, "Come now, and let us *reason* together; *plead* before me." He desires us to state the reasons why we expect he will grant our requests; to appeal to him and put him in remembrance, as a man appeals to his friend; and he often postpones the answer to prayer, to draw out our importunity, after the example of the widow in the parable. We are well aware of the objections unbelievers urge against such statements as these, and which Satan often flings like fiery darts into a Christian's soul. If God is infinitely wise, why need we inform him of our wants? If he is infinitely merciful, why need we plead with him as though he were unwilling to bless us? If he is unchangeable, he has determined already what he will do; why, then, argue our case as though we could move him? Now, we may not be able to solve these difficulties on metaphysical grounds, any more than we can comprehend and explain the mysteries of Eternity, the Trinity, and the Incarnation. But one consideration may satisfy us that they are metaphysical absurdities and temptations from the Father of Lies: they contradict the plain precepts of God, and nullify all his promises. For if they are valid objections against importunate *pleading* with God, they are equally valid against *all* prayer. They are the devices by which Satan and an evil heart of unbelief would wean us entirely from the mercy-seat, and cause us to live in total neglect of the Saviour's example and instructions. Moreover, they proceed upon an entire misapprehension of the nature and design of prayer. It is not meant to instruct, to mollify, or to change the Almighty. His knowledge is perfect, his mercy infinite, his purposes unchangeable. But then the *administration* of his purposes, which in themselves are inscrutable to us as his own nature, is carried on according to certain revealed rules which we can readily understand; and it is one of these rules that he bestows his blessings upon them who ask. "I know the thoughts that I think towards you, saith the Lord, thoughts of peace, and not of evil, to give you an expected end. Then shall ye call upon me, and ye shall go and pray unto me, and I will hearken unto you. And ye shall seek of me, and find me, when ye shall search for me with all your heart." If it be said that the "expected end" and the answer of peace is already fixed in God's purpose, we reply, that the searching with all our heart, on our part, is equally fixed and certain. Though our prayers do not render him merciful nor alter his purposes, yet he will not exercise his mercy towards us without our prayers. The fulness of the reservoir does not depend upon the pipe that conveys the life-giving water to our dwellings; but, without the pipe, that fulness will be of no avail to us. Prayer is the appointed channel, through which the water of eternal life comes to the soul; and it accomplishes its end in proportion to the importunity with which we plead and argue our case before God. It is easy to see the wisdom and love of this divine appointment. With respect to God, prayer is a suitable acknowledgment of our dependence on him. Is it strange that the bountiful Giver should require such acknowledgments from the creatures he has made for his own glory? In respect to ourselves, prayer prepares us to receive his gifts, and enhances our estimate of their value. Though it does not change him, it changes us. Though it is not needful for his information, it is needful to cultivate and testify our submission and gratitude. The gifts of his grace would be wasted, even as his temporal bounties are, if bestowed upon those who will not even ask that they may receive. " It is true the design of the pleading person is not on himself, though the effect is ; neither ought it to be upon God, to move him ; but upon the thing itself, to lay it out before the Lord on the necessity and reasonableness of it. It is as if a hungry child should apply to his father for bread, and the father should say, ' Child, wherefore should I give you bread ? ' and thereupon the child should say, ' Alas ! I am pained with hunger ; and who will give it me, if you refuse ? Will it not be a reflection on your name to say your children lack bread?' While the child pleads thus, the tears gather in his eye, and his earnestness increases: whereupon he is answered. Here it is evident that the effect of the pleading is not on the father, but on the child himself, though he designs it not so."*

Upon a subject so practical as this, facts are better than theories. And how full of facts illustrating the necessity and efficiency of prayer is the word of God! Peniel is a sacred place, and Israel a hallowed name, in the believer's memory † The saints of all ages from Abraham to Christ, Christ himself, and the apostles after him, were all men of prayer. And their example has a special significance in regard to the *arguments* we are to use, when we plead before God. They teach us, even as this doxology does, to enforce our petitions by reasons drawn not from any worthiness in ourselves or in any other creature, but from God alone, from his infinite nature, from his dominion over all things, from his declarative glory. Thus when Daniel pleads for the restoration of Israel, he says: " O my God, incline thine ear, and hear; open thine eyes, and behold our desolations, and the city which is called by thy

* Boston. † Gen. xxxii. 30.

name: for we do not present our supplications before thee for *our* righteousness, but for thy great mercies. O Lord, hear; O Lord, forgive; O Lord, hearken and do; defer not, for *thine own sake*, O my God: for thy city and thy people are called by thy name." So when Abraham pleads for the doomed cities of the plain, he appeals to God's own righteousness; saying, "Peradventure there be fifty righteous within the city: wilt thou also destroy and not spare the place for the fifty righteous that are therein? . . . Shall not the Judge of all the earth do right?" When Moses intercedes between the rebellious people and the divine judgments they had provoked, the burden of his plea and of his anxiety, and the ground of his encouragement, is the *honor* of *God's great name*. He is fearful, if they are destroyed, that the heathen will blaspheme; he hopes that God will glorify the riches of his own grace by sparing them; and therefore he says, "Let the *power of my Lord be great;* and pardon, I beseech thee, the iniquity of the people *according* to the *greatness of thy mercy*." David prayed: "For thy name's sake, O Lord, pardon my iniquity; for it is great." So, David's Lord, when the shadows of the hour and power of darkness began to thicken over him, prayed for himself and for his disciples: "Father, glorify thy name. Glorify thy Son, that thy Son also may glorify thee." And here, in this doxology, he has embodied for us the lessons of all these examples of prayer, and the spirit of his own prevalent intercessions. Neither our righteousness nor our sins, neither our performances nor our sufferings, but the honor of God's own name and the manifestation of his own glory is our plea, when we beseech him to hear us. "*For* thine is the kingdom, and the power, and the glory." How accurately this argument fits on all the foregoing petitions! "Hallowed be thy name," *for thine is the kingdom.* Thou art worthy to reign: all the heavenly hosts adore thee. Oh, hasten the time when the voice of the earth shall mingle without a discord in the praises of the skies! "Thy kingdom come," *for thine is the power;* and not to any human agencies or devices, but to thine own power, do we look for the destruction of Satan's dominion, the extension of the kingdom of grace, and the consummation of that grace in the kingdom of glory. "Thy will be done," *for thine is the glory.* Thy will is perfect; and when it is done here as it is above, the praise shall be altogether thine own.

And so also in regard to the second group of petitions, in which we ask for the supply of our own more immediate wants, the argument of the doxology is beautifully appropriate. We ask and hope to receive " daily bread," because the kingdom of our Father is universal and inexhaustible in its resources. Giving does not impoverish, nor withholding enrich him. We plead for forgiveness, because the gospel is his " power unto salvation to every one that believes : " he is able to save to the uttermost. We supplicate deliverance from the power of temptation and from the dominion of all evil, because it is his glory to save men. Now we give him the praise ; and, when by his grace we are brought off more than conquerors, our voices will swell the everlasting song, " Not unto us, not unto us, but unto thy name, be all the glory, O thou Redeemer of men." While our hearts and lips are filled with such arguments, we expect to be heard; and in token of that expectation we say, AMEN.

www.ingramcontent.com/pod-product-compliance
Lightning Source LLC
Chambersburg PA
CBHW072130160426
43197CB00012B/2059